The Socio-Economic Foundations
of Sustainable Business

Richard Pettinger

The Socio-Economic Foundations of Sustainable Business

Managing in the Fourth Industrial Revolution

Richard Pettinger
School of Management
University College London
London, UK

ISBN 978-3-030-39273-4   ISBN 978-3-030-39274-1 (eBook)
https://doi.org/10.1007/978-3-030-39274-1

© The Editor(s) (if applicable) and The Author(s), under exclusive license to Springer Nature Switzerland AG 2020
This work is subject to copyright. All rights are solely and exclusively licensed by the Publisher, whether the whole or part of the material is concerned, specifically the rights of translation, reprinting, reuse of illustrations, recitation, broadcasting, reproduction on microfilms or in any other physical way, and transmission or information storage and retrieval, electronic adaptation, computer software, or by similar or dissimilar methodology now known or hereafter developed.
The use of general descriptive names, registered names, trademarks, service marks, etc. in this publication does not imply, even in the absence of a specific statement, that such names are exempt from the relevant protective laws and regulations and therefore free for general use.
The publisher, the authors and the editors are safe to assume that the advice and information in this book are believed to be true and accurate at the date of publication. Neither the publisher nor the authors or the editors give a warranty, expressed or implied, with respect to the material contained herein or for any errors or omissions that may have been made. The publisher remains neutral with regard to jurisdictional claims in published maps and institutional affiliations.

Cover illustration: © Melisa Hasan

This Palgrave Pivot imprint is published by the registered company Springer Nature Switzerland AG
The registered company address is: Gewerbestrasse 11, 6330 Cham, Switzerland

Preface

Everywhere in the world there is a revolution going on, a transformation of business and of the products and services needed and wanted by people. At the heart of this revolution are organisations and their leaders and managers. This is underlined by a reality that, whatever was done in the past, and however it was carried out, new ways and new methods are essential for the future. Above all, this means developing a much better understanding of what organisational leadership and management actually are.

The background against which this revolution is taking place is one of economic, social, political and environmental turbulence and upheaval. The global business, political and social environment are unstable and volatile. Ever greater demands and strains are placed on finite and diminishing resources. Globalisation means that production and service delivery activities can now be located anywhere in the world.

This background in underpinned by a technological revolution; and this technological revolution is referred to as the fourth industrial revolution. The first industrial revolution developed mass production techniques and technologies from the mid-eighteenth century onwards; the second was driven by an international arms race from the 1870s, harnessing electrical power en masse for the first time. The third industrial revolution refers to the digitisation and automation of production and IT processes dating from the latter part of the twentieth century. The fourth industrial revolution is building on and developing all of the technological advances of the recent past, making all technologies and IT more or less universally available, and transforming society as well as economic activity and production and service delivery processes. New industries and activities have sprung up; while others have either vanished or else changed forever their ways of working. New social patterns of behaviour are evolving, and these are all supported by business activities; indeed, business provides a universal social infrastructure.

Into all of this comes the effects of the COVID19 pandemic and consequent economic, social and behavioural upheaval of early 2020 and beyond. This book was produced in early 2020. The content then had to be totally revisited to take account of changes to business practices and organisational behaviour that were ordered as the result of great swathes of society across the globe being ordered into lockdown, restraints on travel and physical proximity, and the closure of many businesses and activities that were suddenly deemed to be 'non essential'.

Essential or otherwise, organisations had (and have) to be able to exist and deliver their products, services and service within whatever the operating environment allows. This has meant an immediate and radical shift to online and socially changed working in areas that were not previously considered to need this at all. Others who would 'one day' take advantage of what technology could and might deliver, have had to transform their approaches urgently and immediately if they wanted to stand any chance of remaining viable. The result is that technology and IT are infrastructure by any other name, exactly the same as gas, electricity, water and transport networks.

Marching across all of this are the principles, practice and expertise of leadership and management. The purpose of this book is to set out these principles and the foundations of expert and enduringly effective practice in the present and evolving context.

This book is intended as a reader and foundation for those studying management at undergraduate or postgraduate levels for the first time. It is also a general reader for those already in practice, who are wanting some core material on which to reflect and evaluate.

The approach taken is to revisit the development of the whole field of leadership and management to date, and to set everything in the context of the present day, and the unfolding social, economic and technological environment. With this in mind the book is broken down as follows.

Chapter 1 is called The Foundations of Management sets out the overall present position of the evolution of the principles and expertise of management to date.

Chapter 2 evaluates the social, economic and technological effects of industrial revolutions, and how society changes as the physical and technological infrastructure develops.

Chapter 3 examines the relationship between business and society, and how business development changes collective and individual needs and wants, and how business responds to social pressures and demands. Chapter 4 develops this approach further by examining the disciplines of business from a socio technological perspective. Chapter 5 then broadens this approach still further by examining the environment from a social and behavioural as well as economic point of view.

Chapter 6 takes a fresh and current look at the changing and transient nature of demands for products and services, and how this is changing in a technologically driven and post pandemic world. This is reinforced by evaluating what sustainability is in Chapter 7. Chapter 8 relates this to the need for overall standards of behaviour and conduct, at both organisational and also individual levels.

Chapter 9 evaluates the origins, drives and capacities for technology development, the value that it is supposed to bring, and the immediate and lasting effects on organisations and society.

Chapter 10 provides a review and overview of the foundations of effective and expert leadership, the value that leadership is required to deliver, and the basis on which this expertise is developed.

The final chapter is a conclusion, summarising the overall position and lessons, and also revisiting issues from the past in the development of leadership and management expertise.

Each chapter has a short reading list. These lists are not at all comprehensive; they are intended to open up the subject matter to a wider range of sources so as to develop an ever broadening and deepening knowledge on which to build the leadership and managerial expertise that is so critical to the development of the world for the good of all. Within the chapter content, each subject area clearly feeds off all the others. Good management generates profitable business; profitable business creates and sustains strong organisations and social as well as economic confidence.

The main conclusion to draw is that the whole field of management is constantly expanding, in terms of its social, economic and technological context, both as a field of study and also as area of practice and expertise.

Anyone who aspires to be an excellent and effective manager needs to commit themselves to keeping fully up to date in every aspect of the field. This book is to ensure that those who do aspire to be expert in the field have some key bases from which to work.

July 2020 Richard Pettinger

Acknowledgements

This book has come about in its final form as the result of the great efforts and dedication and commitment of many people. I would like to thank Sarah Warnes for reviewing the manuscript and making sure that the work would be something that we can all be proud of. I am very indebted to Jess Harrison, Anette Weiss, Sham Anand and Srishti Gupta at Palgrave and Springer for all of their support. I am very indebted above all to Balaji Varadharaju at Palgrave and Springer for setting a final schedule to which we could all work, and then making sure that I stuck to it and delivered the different parts when required! This was a truly awesome piece of project management by Balaji all round!

At this stage, I would also like to acknowledge the others with whom I have worked at Palgrave over the years. As well as Jess, Anette, Srishti and Balaji, Susannah Burywood and Ursula Gavin have always been absolutely wonderful to work with and really excellent at all times. There is also the truly great and awe inspiring Stephen Rutt who first got me started as a text book author nearly thirty years ago.

As always, a very great 'thank you' to Kelvin Cheatle, Roger Cartwright, Paul Griseri, Jamie Pollock, Mike Hutton, Ken Batchelor, and Keith Sanders for their total inspiration and support at all times. And finally to my wife Rebecca, without whom nothing would ever have been possible.

Introduction and Overview

This work was produced and finalised during the COVID19 pandemic of 2020; and so it takes account of the great social, economic and technological upheavals that took place in a very short space of time. These upheavals are certain to completely reform the ways in which many business activities are conducted, and to change forever the ways in which organisations are deigned and run, and the social as well as operational patterns of behaviour that everyone was previously familiar with and used to.

In this context, the purpose here is to explore and evaluate the relationship between collective and individual behaviour, society and technology; and from this, to develop knowledge, understanding and the foundations of expertise in a key aspect of business, management and organisation leadership education that to date is little explored or delivered. This then becomes the cornerstone of:

The Socio-Economic Foundations of Sustainable Business

The work on which this book is based had its genesis in working with, and membership of, the UK Tech Partnership and the Information Technology Management for Business (ITMB) venture, which delivered integrated programmes of business, computer science, IT, management and leadership education. Graduates from programmes that include this mix have a 96% chance of gaining a graduate level job and career programme;

and this is observable and referenced across more than 30 top UK and international universities, including the Hasso Plattner Institute at the University of Potsdam, the Jagiellonian and Economics Universities of Krakow, Poland, Singapore Polytechnic and Nanyang University Singapore, West University of Timisoara, Romania, as well as the University College London School of Management. This is in contrast to graduates from mainstream business schools, who have a 44% chance of graduate level employment (exactly the same as non business school graduates).

The work developed in relation to working with such diverse organisations as:

- the Antwerp Diamond Exchange, where the products (the diamonds) are produced to exact and exacting standards of quality and durability in a very highly technologically driven environment and expertise; and where they are then bought and sold on a basis of pure trust and human relationship;
- Daimler—Benz, where the products are produced and delivered almost entirely by technology; however the states of the art of the cars, and how motoring is developing and advancing, is down to the company's ability to hire and engage people on an almost purely human basis also;
- Credit Suisse and Deutsche Bank, both highly technologically driven, and both of which transformed their working culture and approach to business and staffing by adopting human—oriented graduate and staff development schemes;
- Exellys, a Belgian graduate employment company that specialises in hiring, supporting and placing newly qualified graduates into top reputation, high branded, technology driven, IT and computing oriented roles and companies and organisations—but on the basis of their personal qualities and attitudes and commitment, rather than their technological proficiency;
- a myriad of start up companies in London, Paris, Berlin and elsewhere, the most successful of which all took a social as well as economic view of what they were going to do, who for, and how they would serve the best interests of the customer and client bases targeted.

This was all instigated and engaged alongside a review of business school syllabi, outputs, programmes, teaching and learning over the past 20–30 years. Also addressed were iconic and seminal leadership, business and management authors; and this included reviewing the works of Peter Drucker, Tom Peters and Robert Waterman, Nicholas Hayek, Charles Handy, Michael Porter, Kenneth Andrews, C Roland Christensen (and his legacy), as well as many others.

From all of this the following became clear:

- the best business schools delivered (and deliver) syllabi that include IT, computing and entrepreneurship in all programmes;
- in the best business schools, teaching and learning, and assessed courseworks, were as fully integrated with business and management practice and demands;
- in the best business schools also, a substantial number of assessed courseworks were set, delivered and indeed marked in conjunction with companies and organisations;
- there is a core driver in terms of how technologies evolve in relation to organisational, collective and individual behaviour, and vice versa;
- technological proficiency could be taught; however an understanding of people and the 'soft skills' that go with being an effective and influential (as well as expert) human had (and has) to be learned, internalised, understood and applied.

It is essential to know and understand this because of the all-pervasive nature of technology, its effects on business and society, and how this needs to inform leadership, entrepreneurship and management development and expertise.

This is because in every aspect of organisation, work and social life, technology plays an integral part. There is no organisation that is not dependent on technology in some way or another. The ability to recognise this, and the opportunities and constraints that arise as a consequence, are crucial to developing effective business activities, ventures and initiatives. Business viability exists only in its present and evolving environment; and this viability is underpinned by human and social drives as well as economic dependence and integration.

In particular it is essential to be able to evaluate how technologies deliver (and fail to deliver) profitable, effective and valuable products services processes and activities. The standpoint taken is that it is not possible to deliver effective and sustainable business unless there is a wider social benefit and value added, and unless this is factored in to every aspect of business evaluation, planning and development.

In turn it is therefore essential to examine in detail the relationship between society and technology, especially in terms of how and why technologies succeed and fail; the value that technologies deliver (and do not deliver); and the wider position of technology in society.

There are two basic positions from which to start:

- that it is impossible to create effective and sustainable business ventures unless there is a wider contribution to society also;
- that all economic progress depends on activities having and delivering a social as well as economic value.

There is a key relationship between people and technology. This refers especially to how and why individual and collective drives and priorities shape and influence what technologies are valued at any given point. This also refers to how technologies are developed, who controls them, and how they exert that control. There is also a converse: how technologies influence and shape behaviour.

In order to do this, there is a variety of different disciplines on which to draw:

- sociology, in terms of how and why people organise and socialise; the purposes for which societies and communities are drawn together (including business organisations);
- psychology, in terms of understanding perceptions, attitudes and values, and individual and collective drives;
- anthropology, in terms of how and why people organise themselves into social groupings; the fact of organisations as social groupings which have a life, entity and history and aspirations of their own; the history and development of these groupings as social as well as economic entities;
- ethics, in terms of abiding by laws and regulations; delivering and discharging stated and implied responsibilities; and delivering standards and codes of conduct with which everyone agrees to abide;

- economics, in terms of delivering financial and other extrinsic results and performance; and in developing the resource bases for the present and the future on which all activities are going to depend;
- IT and computing, in terms of its universal availability; social as well as economic, business and organisation dependence; and the full integration of IT and computing into every aspect of social as well as economic life;
- maths and analytics, on which all technological, computing, financial and economic development depends; and this includes the ability to evaluate the mathematical results delivered in terms of what is required and demanded by society, organisations, groups and individuals.

This is with a view to synthesising the wider basis and environment in which business, management, entrepreneurial, public service and not-for profit activities take place. This also helps to underpin and explain the following crucial issues:

- technology and technologies delivering social and economic value, collectively and individually;
- the notion of technology and technologies in search of usefulness and value;
- the basis on which human needs, wants, demands and drives in turn influence and shape the demand for new technologies, and shape developments to existing technologies;
- the key roles of individuals and groups in social, economic and organised and ordered settings;
- the need for standards of conduct, behaviour and performance in the present and evolving environment.

This book adds specific knowledge, understanding and the foundations of expertise, in the fields of leadership, management, IT and technology. The book additionally broadens and deepens the wider contextual knowledge and understanding required which is essential in turn in knowing and understanding what is demanded by society in terms of business, organisation, social and economic development.

In this context the book aims to explore and develop the foundations of expert leadership, entrepreneurship and management knowledge and understanding in the following areas:

- the relationship between society and technology, and the effects on businesses and organisations;
- how technologies evolve in relation to organisational, organised, collective and individual behaviour, both in response to human demands, and also in providing new outlets for human and social as well as economic value;
- how technologies deliver (and fail to deliver) profitable, effective and valuable products services processes and activities, and the reasons for this;
- how technologies evolve as the result of social as well as economic demands and pressures;
- how technologies are controlled and directed by human (professional and non-professional) behaviour.

There are some key positions to understand as follows:

- all progress is dependent upon how humans react and respond to their environment;
- what is important and developed is driven by specific human (individual and collective) demands, needs and wants;
- staff management is about maximising and optimising 60–75% of total return on investment;
- people live as well as work in organisations;
- organisations exist in a social as well as economic context and environment;
- the capacity of technology doubles every 18 months (Moore's Law); and this doubling of capacity every 18 months can be traced back at least 5,000 years.

The very few inventions on which all else is based are:

- the wheel;
- shaping and using materials;
- mathematics and astronomy;

- reading and writing;
- harnessing electricity;
- fire and other non-electric sources of energy.

Everything that we have and use is derived from one or more of these sources. Every development is then related to social and economic drives, and to the responses that generate human invention and ingenuity.

Human ingenuity is founded in the need for progress, and this is inherent within humanity, collectively and individually.

Collectively, society and groups of people demand products and services that are of personal, social and economic value, and which enhance every aspect of their lives; and technology and IT are expected to further enhance these products and services, making them ever more valuable, reliable and socially and economically desirable.

Individually, people demand instant and assured gratification, satisfaction and convenience, in whatever terms these issues are defined. On an individual basis, gratification, satisfaction and convenience are defined at every moment of every day; and again, technology is expected and required—and demanded—to be a key part of the infrastructure that delivers, whenever and wherever the question arises.

Contents

1	The Foundations of Management	1
2	Industrial Revolutions	15
3	Business and Society	25
4	The Disciplines of Business	35
5	The Economic Environment	45
6	Products and Services	57
7	Sustainability	69
8	Ethics and Standards	81
9	Technological Development	93

10	**Leadership**	105
11	**Conclusions**	117
Index		127

List of Figures

Fig. 5.1　Open and closed economies　　50
Fig. 6.1　New product and service development process　　63

List of Boxes

Box 2.1	Park Road Fish Bar	17
Box 2.2	The Changing Face and Location of Population Centres	19
Box 2.3	The Changing Nature of the Farming Industry	21
Box 3.1	The Rational/Economic Perspective on Business and Management	27
Box 3.2	Miss-Selling Financial Services Products	30
Box 5.1	Competition at Different Levels	48
Box 6.1	Doing a Ryanair?	58
Box 7.1	Sustainability: Some Definitions	70
Box 7.2	Waste Disposal	72
Box 7.3	Working Remotely	75
Box 7.4	Infrastructure Development	78
Box 9.1	Science Fiction	95
Box 10.1	Leaders and Non-leaders	113

CHAPTER 1

The Foundations of Management

Abstract This chapter summarises the foundations of management knowledge and expertise so as to provide a foundation and context for the rest of the book. This is defined from the point of view of what is a more or less agreed body of knowledge and expertise as established to date. This is then in turn set in the context of the world as it is at present, with especial reference to the restructuring of businesses, business and the economic and social world order as it emerges from the COVID19 pandemic.

Keywords Foundations of management · Moore's law · Leadership · People · Profit · Resources · Improvement · Change · Environment · Technology · Finance · Risk · Profession

As stated in the preface, the overall purpose is to explore and develop the foundations of expert leadership, entrepreneurship and management knowledge and understanding in the following areas:

- the relationship between society and technology, and the effects on businesses and organisations;
- the fact of business and businesses providing the core of the social infrastructure on which we all depend;

- how technologies evolve in relation to organisational, organised, collective and individual behaviour, both in response to human demands, and also in providing new outlets for human and social as well as economic value;
- how technologies deliver (and fail to deliver) profitable, effective and valuable products services processes and activities, and the reasons for this;
- how technologies evolve as the result of social as well as economic demands and pressures;
- how technologies are controlled and directed by human (professional and non-professional) behaviour.

These are key issues for anyone in leadership, management, executive and other key positions. These are key issues also for entrepreneurs. These issues are then set in the following context:

- all progress is dependent upon how humans react and respond to their environment;
- what is important and developed is driven by specific human (individual and collective) demands, needs and wants;
- staff management is about maximising and optimising 60–75% of total return on investment;
- people live as well as work in organisations; and so organisations are social as well as technological and economic and productive entities;
- organisations exist in a social as well as economic context and environment;
- the capacity of technology doubles every 18–24 months (Moore's Law); and this doubling of capacity every 18–24 months can be traced back at least 5000 years.

Every development is then related to social and economic drives, and to the responses that generate human invention and ingenuity. As above, human ingenuity is founded in the need for progress, and this is inherent within humanity, collectively and individually.

Collectively, society and groups of people demand products and services that are of personal, social and economic value, and which enhance every aspect of their lives; and technology and IT are expected to further enhance these products and services, making them ever more valuable, reliable and socially and economically desirable.

Individually, people demand instant and assured gratification, satisfaction and convenience, in whatever terms these issues are defined. On an individual basis, gratification, satisfaction and convenience are defined at every moment of every day; and again, technology is expected and required—and demanded—to be a key part of the infrastructure that delivers, whenever and wherever the question arises.

Leadership and Management

In this context, 'management' is a body of knowledge, skills and expertise which must be applied in ways demanded by the particular organisation in which the individual manager is working; and in ways demanded also by the particular environment in which activities are being conducted. Leadership expertise is a key part of management. This expertise is founded in knowledge and understanding of the following:

- achieving things through people;
- achieving things for people;
- making a profit and delivering performance;
- using scarce resources; and planning, organising, controlling and accounting for resources;
- improving and developing products, services, service and processes;
- coping with change and uncertainty;
- environment knowledge and understanding, and working within the constraints of the environment;
- setting collective and individual standards of conduct, behaviour and performance;
- technological knowledge and understanding;
- financial knowledge and understanding;
- risk knowledge and understanding;
- providing leadership expertise and capability.

This knowledge, understanding and expertise has to be applied on a varying and contextual basis, both in terms of the organisation for which the work is carried out and the expertise applied, and also in terms of the daily situations in which individual managers find themselves.

Leadership and management are carried out in and on behalf of organisations; and organisations operate in their environment. Organisations have their own life, direction, legal status, permanence and identity; and are energised by people, and their expertise, skills, talents and commitment.

Clearly, many organisations do still need to command huge and expensive premises, offices, factories, hospitals, shops, airports and other facilities. There is nothing wrong with this (indeed there is everything right with it) so long as the structure remains a matter of constant review; so long as the resource bases can sustain it; and so long as it continues to be as fully effective as possible in terms of serving its purposes overall. Fixed premises provide often critical opportunities for substantial business development.

However, the primary purposes of product and services delivery, and service excellence, have caused leaders, entrepreneurs and managers to look at alternative means of 'organising'. For example:

- federated and virtual organisations depend entirely on their people working from home, the car, flexible locations, business centres and hotel facilities;
- some organisations develop and sustain highly profitable business wholly or mainly through social media;
- some organisations are able to place all of their business processes and functions online; and this means that there is no need for anything but a very small core and often flexible use of premises.

Whatever form of organisation is chosen or demanded, the key factors remain the ability to produce and deliver the required volumes of products and services to every customer or client who needs or wants them, in the volumes and quality needed and expected. So long as this is achieved, any and every form of organisation may be effective in its own terms. The form of organisation chosen also provides the context for the key management tasks and priorities, as above and as follows.

ACHIEVING THINGS THROUGH PEOPLE

At the core of this is the need to maximise and optimise the return on investment in the staff; staff costs normally account for between 60 and 75% of working capital. Achieving things through people is a key priority because no managerial activity takes place in isolation from staff and their expertise. The capabilities, commitment and willingness of people have to be harnessed in ways that are of value to the organisation. To do this effectively requires a knowledge and understanding of organisational, collective and individual human behaviour, with especial reference to how people act and react in particular situations and circumstances; and how people act and react in response to specific incidents and events, and to crises, emergencies and change.

Achieving Things for People

Achieving things for people, in particular meeting and responding to the legitimate demands and expectations of customers, suppliers and shareholders, is also essential. The requirements of everyone involved must be satisfied or else the customers will go elsewhere, suppliers will seek other outlets for their materials and expertise, and backers will seek alternative organisations and ventures in which to invest.

Customers require confidence in the products and services on offer. Customers require that their demands for quality, durability and volumes of products and services are met. Customers expect to be able to return to the company or organisation for product and service upgrades, maintenance, replacement and repairs.

Suppliers require steady and known volumes of business; and so they will gravitate towards those organisations that deliver this on long term and more or less assured bases.

Shareholders and other backers and financial interests require assured levels of returns, both in share values and also in dividend repayments, as a prerequisite to investment.

Achieving things for people is therefore based on a combination of effective organisation, together with the confidence and assurance that comes from producing and delivering excellent and profitable products and services.

Making a Profit

All organisations must make a profit. 'Profit' needs to be defined by all organisations and their managers in their own terms. Profit is composed of the following elements:

- Surplus of income over expenditure, which requires full and detailed knowledge and understanding of product and service surpluses and losses; and also to include surpluses and losses per location and per customer;
- Organisational reputation and confidence, as the result of the ways in which products and services are delivered, as well as attention to absolute expectations in meeting product, and service volume and quality demands;
- Costs, cost effectiveness and cost efficiency; efficient and effective cost management can lead to a much greater income margin per product and service.

The 'profit' delivered by public service organisations is a function of the speed, effectiveness and completeness of service delivery, as well as the ability to stay within financial and other resource constraints. The profit delivered by public services is directly influenced by their ability to respond to: political directives; gain income from external sources (e.g. hospitals selling flowers and books for the patients and other relatives); and develop their services according to particular local and environmental needs (e.g. schools providing evening classes, sports' clubs and playgroups outside normal hours).

The 'profit' delivered by not-for-profit organisations and charities is a function of the extent to which they can, and do, raise the levels of funding and resources required to serve the particular client bases. Not-for-profit work also takes place in a competitive environment. Consequently, those responsible for the management of foundations and charities have to arrive at a clear view as to whether they are competing with other charities (e.g. 'If people give to me, they will not give to others'); or whether people will give anyway (e.g. competing for customer's disposable income overall).

Using Scarce Resources

Managers are required to organise, prioritise, use and consume—and produce a return on—those resources that are placed at their disposal. Resources may be:

- usable once only (e.g. individual components of products);
- reusable (e.g. staff expertise; production technology);
- commoditised (e.g. databases and customer information may be sold to others as well as used oneself);
- improvable (e.g. databases and the ways in which data is analysed are constantly being developed and made more accurate).

All resources are ultimately finite; and even where resources are plentiful and assured for the present and foreseeable future, they should be used and consumed as efficiently and as effectively as possible.

Organisation production, service and information technology, property, premises and equipment, are resources with capital and operational values. This value may be expressed in direct financial terms (i.e. how much would be realised were these factors to be sold off); and in derived terms (i.e. how much they contribute to overall performance and also to specific activities).

Data and databases are resources, with capital and operational values. Databases inform customer and client interactions. As above, databases may be capable of commoditisation if the data held is of value to others for any reason.

Staff expertise, willingness and commitment are resources. Expertise and commitment are both required; neither is effective in isolation from the other. Organisations that have staff expertise and commitment, targeted at known, understood and agreed priorities, out-perform those that do not. Organisations that have expertise but no commitment or engagement lose staff to other organisations where there is a greater sense of overall purpose.

Improvement

Everything that is done in organisations and by people is capable of improvement; and in turn, improvement is demanded in every area of activity and process. Customers and clients expect improved products and services. Staff expect improved wages, salaries, terms and conditions of employment; improvements in the quality of their working environment and working relationships; and improved opportunities and interest in their job and careers. Shareholders and financial interests expect improved returns on their investments.

The demand for improvement is a fundamental human as well as organisational need. Managers must therefore seek to improve processes, attitudes and behaviour, as well as products, services and outputs.

COPING WITH CHANGE AND UNCERTAINTY

Coping with change and uncertainty requires a full and detailed knowledge and understanding of the organisation; the operating environment; the products and services; and the staff and their priorities, hopes, fears and expectations.

Especially, it is essential to know and understand, and be able to respond to, the effects of the following:

- natural disasters including earthquakes, floods and drought;
- economic, social and political crises brought on by e.g.: pandemics; stock market crashes; runs on particular currencies (and upward valuations of others); energy crises and energy shocks and shortages;
- market crises brought about by losses in consumer, wholesaler and investor confidence;
- market and activity shifts brought about by the availability of expertise and technology in different parts of the world, enabling entry to markets and activities on a much wider scale than before;
- new technology may render existing technologies obsolete;
- the amount of market share taken by new entrants;
- product and services defects and faults;
- website and technology crashes;
- lack of availability of expertise.

Change and uncertainty remain constant features in the employment of staff. The stability, commitment and engagement of the staff and workforce are never fully assured, however good the wages, terms and conditions and managerial and supervisory style and relations may be. All organisations to be aware of: the value of their approaches to staff development; the effects of new employers (especially large employers) moving into the area; the effects of large employers leaving the area; increases in demand for relatively mobile staff (e.g. professionally qualified people) elsewhere; and gaining and losing road, rail and air infrastructure and transport connections.

Environment Knowledge and Understanding

Environment knowledge and understanding are essential because every manager needs to be expert in the operating conditions under which they are working (see Chapter 3). Environment knowledge and understanding inform every aspect of management and leadership practice:

- scanning for opportunities and threats;
- technological and IT developments and opportunities;
- organisations in their physical and built environments;
- the interrelationships of different technologies, operating and IT systems;
- project management and project planning;
- risk and its management;
- sources of staff and competition for staff;
- sources of other resources and competition for other resources;
- changes to social structures in given locations;
- other social and economic activities in give locations.

Each of these elements forms the basis of knowing and understanding the social and operating environment, and where the external pressures are likely to come from. It is also essential from the point of view of ensuring that there is a good fit between organisations and their environment, and that companies are going to be comfortable at a human as well as operating level, as they conduct their activities.

Technological Knowledge and Understanding

Technological knowledge and understanding are essential from the points of view of:

- knowing its capability and capacity; and knowing what it can and cannot do;
- knowing and understanding the pressures under which those who operate it have work;
- knowing the cost, nature and value of the expertise that it needs to make it work;
- knowing the costs and scheduling of maintenance and upgrade;

- understanding key issues around safety, access, security and data and information assurance;
- knowing the likely and possible length of useful life before it needs to be replaced;
- knowing and understanding the full range of resources required to ensure that it operates to maximum and optimum capacity.

Managers need to adopt attitudes and approaches based on the fact that it may be necessary to change technologies and information systems at any time because of sudden obsolescence or new and better technologies suddenly becoming available.

Financial Knowledge and Understanding

Financial knowledge and understanding are essential because everything is founded in the capability and willingness to pay for every activity. If activities are not financially resourced, they cannot go ahead. Managers have to be able to assess their own overall financial needs. They have to be able to allocate budgets and other resources, and account for them as they are used. Managers have to be able to evaluate the costs and benefits of specific activities. Managers have to be able to plan in financial terms for everything that they are doing and planning. Managers have to be able to convince their own seniors, and this normally means being able to debate specific issues in financial terms. Managers therefore need specific knowledge and understanding as follows:

- budgeting, forecasting and estimating;
- costing of specific activities;
- costing of overall activities within the constraints placed by the organisation and its systems and processes;
- business and project planning;
- maintenance scheduling and planning;
- contingency and crisis funding.

Financial management is a continuous process. Finance needs to be monitored and evaluated continuously as a part of professional practice so that any issues and concerns are raised and addressed immediately.

Risk Knowledge and Understanding

Risk knowledge and understanding are essential because there is an ever-greater awareness that risk and issues continue to occur in spite of the more or less universal existence of risk management policies. At every level of organisation, collective and individual activities there are statutory and organisational risk management policies, which have to be addressed and understood and signed off before anything can take place or be undertaken.

It is essential to understand the centrality of human behaviour in risk and its management as follows. The main causes of things going wrong are:

- complacency and laziness;
- not seeing or valuing the importance of risk and its management;
- personal choice to attend or not to attend to risky situations and events;
- knowing that ultimate responsibility and accountability lie elsewhere.

These patterns of behaviour have to be recognised and addressed and then managed out of any situation where they exist.

Leadership Capability

Every manager needs leadership capability. Leadership capability is the combination of persuading, inspiring and motivating others to work in particular ways and to engage willingly with the interests of the organisation or entity that is being led. Top and senior managers will spend high proportions of their time in leadership activities. With very few exceptions, entrepreneurs will lead their new ventures, at least until the idea and the organisation have grown to the point where other forms of direction may be required.

Leadership takes place in relation to people. People come to those in leadership positions for advice, guidance, direction, permission and help. It follows from this that a key part of the manager's role is meeting and interacting and communicating with people, addressing their problems, concerns, hopes, fears, ambitions and aspirations. This is additionally and crucially a key part of ensuring the maximum return on investment in the staff.

Management as Profession

The detailed knowledge, understanding and expertise detailed above is wide ranging and critical to the success of organisations and business ventures. Those who aspire to this expertise have therefore to take a fully committed and professional approach to their work, their capabilities and the ways in which they live their lives.

However, in traditional terms, management is not (yet) a profession because it has none of the features that professions are always deemed to have. The 'true professions' are normally deemed to be: law, medicine; religious priesthood; and soldiering. These true professions all have the following:

- prequalifications which must be held as a condition of appointment or practice;
- a regulatory body to which every person in the profession must answer;
- codes of conduct which transcend any organisational demands;
- self-regulation, self-determination and self-discipline;
- specific standards of conduct and behaviour;
- a commitment to wider service, delivering the profession and its expertise for the greater good, as well as for the person who is paying;
- commitment to a morality, moral compass and work ethic;
- the ability to set charges, costs and fees independently;
- a commitment to continuous professional development;
- the ability to choose whom to work for; and the ability to choose whom not to work for;
- the ability to choose when to work, and when not to work.

Clearly management has still some way to go before it reaches this stage and level of recognition. However this does not preclude any manager from taking a fully 'professional' approach to everything that they do. Especially, all aspiring professional and expert managers need to commit themselves to:

- continuous professional development;
- continuous environmental scanning, for developments, opportunities and risks;

- establishing and delivering their own morality, standards and moral compass;
- leading and managing by example.

Especially, all managers need to establish standards of conduct, behaviour and performance, based on fundamental equality and equity of treatment and respect for all. Managers have to be clear about the attitudes and behaviour that they demand and encourage; and they have to be clear about what they will not tolerate and will punish if they find it occurring at all.

Conclusions

The overall purpose here has been to illustrate the complexity, range and scale of the subject-matter that is to be considered, the widely differing standpoints from which it has been tackled, and the progression of it as a field of study.

A summary of the foundations of management in this way clearly illustrates the range of skills, knowledge, understanding and expertise involved. For those who aspire to be truly expert leaders, entrepreneurs and managers, delivering effective products and services in whatever organisation and circumstances they may find themselves, there is no substitute for acquiring and developing this range of skills, knowledge, understanding and expertise.

It is additionally critical to note that much of the pressure that exists on and in companies and organisations at present has arisen (and continues to arise) because of the lack of managerial expertise and an understanding of what makes companies and organisations effective and profitable, and how to get staff to do the right things at the right time. The banking and political crises of the period since 2008 arose because of decisions taken by leaders and managers; these crises did not cause themselves to happen. The COVID19 crisis of 2020 is being dealt with by leaders and managers; this crisis did not cause itself to happen.

There have therefore to be other ways of doing things, that ensure enduring viability and profitability in the present and evolving environment; and this has to be a major challenge for those who are to lead, direct and manage organisations in all sectors and locations for the future.

REFERENCES AND FURTHER READING

Branson, R. 1994. *Losing My Virginity*. Virgin Publishing.
Drucker, P. 1999. *Management Challenges for the Twenty First Century*. HarperCollins.
Hammer, M., and Champy, J. 1996. *Reengineering the Corporation*. Harvard.
Handy, C. 2004. *Understanding Organisations*. Penguin.
Kanter, R.M. 1998. *The Change Masters*. Free Press.
Peters, T. 1992. *Liberation Management*. Pan.
Peters, T.J., and Waterman, R.H. 1982. *In Search of Excellence*. Harper and Row.
Pettinger, R. 2007. *Introduction to Management*, 4th ed. Palgrave.
Pugh, D., and Hickson, D. 1973. *Writers on Organisations*. Penguin Business.
Simon, H. 1967. *Organisations*. Harper and Row.

CHAPTER 2

Industrial Revolutions

Abstract This chapter defines the economic and social structures that have emerged from the industrial revolutions that have shaped society and the structures of business and organisation to date. The structures are summarised in organisational and social terms. In turn the economic drives and foundations are defined in relation to organisational and social needs, wants and demands.

Keywords Industrial revolutions · Pandemic · Political changes · Social revolutions · Infrastructure · Technology · IT · Industrial evolution · Disruption · Data

Introduction

Everywhere in the world there are business and organisational revolutions going on, as company and public service leaders and managers seek to develop ever new and better ways of conducting their affairs, producing and delivering products and services, and gaining increased usage from scarce and very often expensive resources. These revolutions are being further energised and driven by a range of key and current and permanent changes to what was considered to be an assured and more or less certain social, political and economic world order:

© The Author(s) 2020
R. Pettinger, *The Socio-Economic Foundations of Sustainable Business*,
https://doi.org/10.1007/978-3-030-39274-1_2

- The COVID19 pandemic;
- Political changes and repositioning are driven in different parts of the world by: the US presidency; Brexit; 5G and the companies driving it; political repositioning in Russia and South America;
- Technological advances and developments in every field of political, social and economic activity;
- The amounts of data that are gathered, stored and used, and the purposes for which the data is used;
- The advantages and disadvantages of global—and local—supply chains.

As old and traditional markets and ways of doing things pass along, new prospects and opportunities constantly open up and become apparent. This is causing everyone in any executive position at all to take an ever broader view of how to organise work, where to locate businesses and business activities, and how to deliver products and services.

Everywhere in the world there are social revolutions going on also. These revolutions are driven by a combination of:

- developments in the transport and communications infrastructures that have enabled people in any part of the world to get to work with others wherever and whenever they choose;
- wars and political upheavals which cause people to migrate to safer and more stable locations;
- climate change and its consequences, rendering parts of the world either virtually uninhabitable, or else forcing changes to life patterns and structures;
- development of current industrial revolutions in 'emerging nations', and which are bringing about social revolutions alongside the economic and industrial developments.

This is all underpinned by the present and constantly evolving IT and technology infrastructure; and this infrastructure is now more or less universally available. What was previously only available to small and exclusive areas and activities is now completely mainstream and familiar to all—and is becoming essential for social, economic and personal activities in all areas.

Technology is at the forefront of all organisational, business and social development. Technology and the IT infrastructure now support every aspect of life. Essential and near essentials including water, electricity supply, and the energy, transport and telecommunications sectors are now fully technology driven. Public services, including health, education and social care, are now technology informed and technology driven, in their delivery to their clients and user groups. Other sectors including fast moving consumer goods (FMCG), and food and drink production and distribution, are also wholly or mainly dependent on technology to energise the ways in which people are able to access them. Indeed it is very difficult to find any organisation in any sector or location that does not depend to a greater extent on technology for its overall wellbeing (see Box 2.1).

Box 2.1 Park Road Fish Bar

The Park Road Fish Bar is a single site family owned fish and chips shop in a small town in south east England. It sells traditional English fish and chips; and as with all other such retailers, offers pies, sausages, burgers and fritters as variations. It looks very much like a very traditional and familiar operation all-round.

It is also a fully technologically driven operation. Park Road Fish Bar has technology and IT systems that regulate and inform every activity, as follows:

- the length of time that the frying fat can be used before it needs to be changed;
- the temperatures required to cook particular food in accordance with regulations;
- the levels of stock that have to be carried in order to be able to satisfy demand with the minimum of wastage;
- the length of time that cooked and prepared foods can be held before they have to be thrown away if not sold.

Park Road Fish Bar also uses technology to manage its finances. The payment and till systems record all income and expenditure; and these systems are tied to the operational bank account. The systems identify possible and potential cash flow difficulties, allowing a fully open and informed relationship with the bank. This approach also enables fully

> informed and supported discussions with suppliers and energy and utility companies to take place if every necessary.
> Park Road Fish Bar also belongs to a range of local social media networks, as well as to Uber and Just Eat, bringing in about £1200 per week from customers who would not otherwise be able to order or collect easily.
> The purpose of this example is to underpin the assertion that every organisation is to some extent technologically driven. The example also illustrates—at a very local level—just how much influence technology has on every aspect of business conduct; and by extrapolation, it illustrates the need for everyone to be as technologically informed and capable as possible. It also reflects the ways in which business is conducted at all levels: companies are expected to deliver products, services and processes via technology; and people expect the convenience of choice when ordering their goods and services.

Industrial Revolutions

Industrial revolutions take place as inventions, technologies, transport and communication networks come together to deliver fundamentally different methods of production and service delivery, which overtake and make obsolete the existing and familiar patterns of work and operations.

Industrial revolutions act additionally as drivers of social change, in that the economic and industrial institutions demand changes to social, working, living and non-work activities. Developments of population clusters, towns, cities, ports and airports deliver in turn changes to the physical environment and social structures. People's habits, patterns of life, social networks and collective and individual behaviour all change, both in response to the developments of the physical environment, and also in terms of the opportunities for further development that the evolving physical environment delivers.

Industrial revolutions deliver essential services in response to social demands and drives. 'Essential services' are those services believed and perceived to be essential or highly desirable to maintaining and improving the quality of life in the given locations. These services include the developments of healthcare, education, security, policing and legal structures and authorities; and they also include transport, energy, water and telecommunications infrastructures, to be used by everyone both as a part of the social fabric, and also whenever required by the members of the communities.

Industrial evolution takes place at all times. Industrial revolutions take place when there is a cataclysmic social, economic and technological mix that comes to pass in specific societies and locations, and which then drives a much wider and far reaching change to the existing social order. As well as developing the economic and financial outputs of production and service delivery, industrial revolutions change social habits, human behaviour, the physical and built environment, and collective and individual human interaction. Industrial evolution builds on the revolutions and upheavals, maintaining and improving what is now in existence in terms of social, economic and technological structures and circumstances.

At the core of these events is technology and its effects on collective and individual behaviour, aspiration, ambition and opportunity. As well as providing the foundations for individual and collective economic and social development and advancement, it delivers wider and critical parts of social and industrial infrastructure; and this then in turn becomes the foundation for further progress and development (see Box 2.2).

Box 2.2 The Changing Face and Location of Population Centres
The changing face of cities and societies is illustrated in this moving graphic. This illustrates especially how the movements of people to and from specific locations, affects physical size of locations. It follows from this that as population centres become larger, they create the need for support activities, supply chains and services, as well as developing the core business and industries for which people moved in the first place https://www.facebook.com/yevgeny.gindilis/videos/10213295025185704/.

As above, industrial revolutions and evolution go on all over the world. In the western world, there are understood to have been four industrial revolutions.

The first industrial revolution is held to have commenced in the mid-eighteenth century. Its key feature was that it led to the mechanisation of many industrial activities that had hitherto been carried out by individuals. It was characterised by the development of machines to produce more and better products more cheaply and efficiently, and to universal standards. It was also characterised by the early developments of road, waterway and railway transport infrastructure and networks for the transportation of goods and people cheaply and efficiently.

The second industrial revolution is held to be dated 1870–1914. It was founded in the development of key features of mass production, motorisation and the further development of roads and railways across great swathes of countries. At the core of this revolution was an international arms race, created and perpetuated by the UK, France, Germany, Russia and the USA. The arms race especially led to the development of machines and associated expertise that could very easily be transposed into the production of socially desirable and valuable products.

The second industrial revolution came to a cataclysmic head in 1914 with the outbreak of the First World War. While political history states that this war was caused by a chain of events in central Europe, social evaluation is clear that the arms race powers were driving at finding reasons to try out their new and industrially produced weapons. This would then in turn lead to future developments of even more effective weapons and military technology; and this too would have spin offs for the development of commercial and more mainstream products services and enhancements over the future.

The third industrial revolution is perceived to date from the 1980s and relates to the digital revolution. This is characterised by the capability to digitise and standardise products, services and communications. Its core components are the invention and development of the internet and World Wide Web, and the widespread provision of, and access to, computing, telecommunications and personal as well as industrial information management and data processing technology. Digitisation has also revolutionised production process and service delivery.

The fourth industrial revolution is held to be that in which we find ourselves today. It reflects the more or less universal availability of technology, and the ways in which it is embedded in every aspect of society, economic and social activities. Everyone now has (actual and potential) access to hardware and software for economic, work, social and entertainment purposes. Additionally the fourth industrial revolution has led—and is leading—to major advances (and the consequent economic, social and organisational disruption) in biometrics, health care, travel and transport,

Each of these revolutions has lasting social impacts. These impacts have laid the foundations of society—and business, today and for the foreseeable future. Some key features are:

- urbanisation, and the shift away from small subsistence communities to larger economic communities;
- the shift from agrarian and industrial subsistence to wage—work bargains and the development of companies and organisations;
- the shift to mass employment and the communities created by masses of workers;
- development of primary (mining and extraction), secondary (manufacturing) and tertiary (services) industrial and commercial sectors;
- the development of industries and services that support the urbanisation process;
- the development of universally accessible transport, utility, electricity/energy, communications and travel networks;
- the development of public and socially driven services;
- the development of services that support the interlinking of the urban (and non-urban) centres.

In their own time, these were and are major social and psychological upheavals, as well as being at the core of economic advance. All this led (and is leading) to the repositioning of society into towns and cities; and this repositioning continues today in the fourth industrial revolution, as new and technology driven infrastructure, networks, communities, cities and towns open up (see Box 2.3).

Box 2.3 The Changing Nature of the Farming Industry

The infrastructure that was first developed during the first industrial revolution has left its mark to this day in terms of the location and nature of cities, the road and rail networks and the distribution of energy and water.

Along the route networks and in the associated towns and cities, opportunities for further development opened up (and continue to open up to this day). The critical factor is transport; everywhere needs to be able to make and accept deliveries, goods and services. If it is not possible to deliver essentials of food, drink, electricity, water supplies and essential services such as health care, then communities will die out. It is also essential to note that communities have to have an economic as well as social reason for being: if work is not provided and made valuable and meaningful, then again communities will die out.

Consequently, many rural communities die out because the reason for their existence disappears. In the past such communities delivered labour

> intensive farming activities, providing work for everyone in the locality. With the mechanisation of farming activities, and the development of farming organisations from family concerns into large organisations, the traditional work has been lost. Such communities have therefore had to evolve or else die out. The consequences were (and are):
>
> - people have moved away to seek other opportunities elsewhere;
> - those who remain have to generate their own economic support, invariably by commuting elsewhere to work;
> - those who seek to remain start up their own business and enterprises, very often developing new and hitherto untried activities in particular locations;
> - those who seek to remain find work in public and other essential or desirable services in particular locations;
> - those who wish to remain in farming have to adapt to the standards and structures that go with the farming industry in its present form;
> - those who wish to remain have to work within the present social, technological and economic structures of the industry.

Social and Economic Disruption

Developments and advances in technology and IT cause social and economic disruption. On the one hand, this is self-evident; on the other hand, social and economic disruptions have always been by-products of industrial revolutions. It is also the case that if it is not in people's interests to change their habits alongside the technological advances, then they will not do so.

For the fourth and present industrial revolution, some of this disruption is noted for the first time as a combination of fashion and excitement (e.g. being an early customer of Amazon; being an early supplier of online services). Some of this disruption also is noted as being inconvenient and a barrier to progress (e.g. automated telephone answering systems). Some IT services do not always give out a point of physical or telephone contact if customers have questions that they need to have addressed, and this too is a departure from the habits formed over many years. However, the range of opportunities opened up, and the convenience that IT and technology is known, believed and perceived to bring, mean that the overwhelming pressure is to go forward and not back.

In terms of the fourth industrial revolution also, technology and IT developments are all part of a process of continuous development and evolution. One invention may not lead to revolutionary change; however it may (and very often does) contribute to further developments which do at specific points bring about transformative and radical new approaches to products, services, service and markets.

The continuous development of technology is common to all industrial revolutions. However a key factor to note in terms of the fourth industrial revolution is the speed of technological advance; and this is a feature that is unique to the fourth industrial revolution. As above, Moores' Law states that the capacity of technology doubles every eighteen months; IBM state that the amount of data generated between 'big bang' and 2015, is to double by 2022, and double again by 2027. The overall pressure that this speed of development brings about is not easy to resist.

Overall, people at least acquiesce in relation to the opportunities brought about by technological advances. Some of those who do not acquiesce simply reject it, preferring to use the old ways. Others tend to be 'wait and see – ers' who delay adopting until the particular value has been proven, or else until early glitches have been ironed out. The overall effect is that a very great many inventions and developments very quickly gain a life of their own; and in turn any value delivered (or otherwise) very quickly becomes apparent also.

Conclusions

It is apparent from all of the above that concentrating only on the technology is certain to ensure that its potential is not maximised. Technology has to either facilitate the delivery of value, or else deliver value itself. On the other hand, concentrating only on behaviour ignores that fact that all organisations are constituted for a purpose. Evaluating and understanding the nature of the present industrial revolution in full detail, and identifying and analysing the changes in opportunities that it is delivering, is a sound basis for understanding in the fullest possible detail the present and envisaged context of what business and businesses are likely to be able to deliver.

Additionally and crucially, technology, industrial revolution and social evolution are being ever more energised by the COVID19 pandemic of 2020 and beyond. Restrictions on travel and social as well as economic activity are causing everyone to look at the developments that technology can bring. This affects every aspect of human life, and is changing organisation, economic and social structures and behaviour.

More generally, these advances and opportunities fuel collective and individual ambitions to be a part of them, and to drive and shape and influence either what is going on, or else what could be going on. From this point of view, technological and business developments collectively influence and enhance society, and the experiences of everyone. They provide in turn the context and basis for all organisational and entrepreneurial activity, and also crucially deliver individual opportunities and potential for ambition and achievement, both for new start-up companies, and also for established global organisations in every sphere of activity and industry. These actions are only going to be fully effective, however technology and society evolve, if businesses set out to address social and psychological needs as well as economic drives.

REFERENCES AND FURTHER READING

Abrudan, D. (ed). 2018. *Performing Organisations*. Gower Press.
Berg, B., and P. Silvia. 2012. *Introducing HANA*. SAP IBM Publications.
Braun, E. 2014. *Futile Progress: Technology's Empty Promise*. Earthscan.
Christensen, C., and J. Bower. 1995. *Disruptive Technologies: Catching the Wave*. Harvard Business Review, January–February.
Doane, M. 2015. *The SAP Green Book*. Galileo.
Drucker, P.F. 1999. *Management Challenges for the 21st-Century*. HarperCollins.
Ernst and Young. 2016. *Performance Technology: Accelerating Business Performance*. www.uk.ey.com/advisory.
Handy, C.B. 1996. *The Empty Raincoat*. Penguin.
IBM. 2015. *IBM Watson: Towards a Comprehensive Data Management System*. www.UK.IBM.com.
Lessem, R.S. 1990. *Global Management Principles*. Prentice Hall International.
Sullivan, G. 2011. *The SAP Project: More than a Survival Guide*. Galileo.
Tawney, R.H. 2011. *Religion and the Rise of Capitalism*. Penguin.
UKSPA. 2017. *Innovation into Success: Building, Technology, Business*. Reed Elsevier.
Valachich, J., and C. Schneider. 2013. *Information Systems Today: Managing in the Digital World*. Pearson.

CHAPTER 3

Business and Society

Abstract This chapter gives an overview of how society evolves as a result of industrial and economic advances and changes. The purpose is to define the social and technological infrastructure, needs, wants and demands that have to be in place if the society is to survive and flourish. It is not enough simply to provide the means of economic activity; quality of life has to be present also. It follows from this that much of business and economic development takes place in order to develop and underpin the quality of life demanded.

Keywords Business and society · Fourth industrial revolution · Infrastructure · Rational/economic perspective · Quality of life

Introduction

The purpose of this chapter is to evaluate the effects that industrial revolutions have had on society and technology, as well as on the evolution of the business and social infrastructure that have occurred as the result. It is essential to know and understand the overall basis for the development of successful and effective business and businesses; and this is only possible if there is a good understanding of how and why the social and economic infrastructure exists as it does.

The Fourth Industrial Revolution

As stated in Chapter 2 above, the fourth industrial revolution is deemed to be going on at the present time; and it is certain to be the foundations of all business, commercial, economic and social activity for the foreseeable future.

As above also, all businesses use technology, and are driven and energised by technology, to a greater or lesser extent. Every human life is organised and driven—and served—by technology to a greater or lesser extent. Every social, economic and personal interaction is served and underpinned by technology.

Towns and cities themselves in turn create their own social, economic and technological infrastructures, leading to further developments in terms of:

- creation of mass social, economic and service organisations;
- creation of masses of small companies and organisations;
- creation of transport and other social and economic integration infrastructure that enables people to go about their working, social and daily lives;
- creation of an infrastructure that supports every aspect of life: health care, social care, transport, communications, domestic life and entertainment.

While this is centred on technology, the usage drives are social and behavioural (for which there is an economic return assumed and required). It is therefore essential to know and understand the extent to which each of these events and everything that goes on within them influences everything that is devised, developed, conducted, produced and delivered by organisations. It is additionally essential to understand that a lot of technology advance is driven by choices and wants, rather than needs: for example:

- Amazon and its services are driven by demands for convenience and ease of access (want not need), to products and services that are choices rather than essentials;
- Ryanair and the low-cost air travel sector is driven by the ability and willingness of people to choose particular destinations for short breaks and other visits;

- ASOS is driven by the demand for cheap and fashionable clothing; and while being clothed is essential (socially as well as in terms of personal survival), choosing particular designs relates to want not need;
- Uber is a choice to be made when deciding how to be transported in particular locations.

Each of the above examples relates to the human aspects of being in society at the present day, as well as driving new and ground breaking business opportunities. It is therefore essential to know and understand the main disciplines that now contribute extensively to how the fourth industrial revolution is developing, and the reasons for these developments.

Developing the Knowledge Base

If people are to be successful and effective in the present environment, then it is necessary to broaden the base of leadership and management knowledge and understanding. Traditionally, the disciplines of business and management were taught, learned and mastered from a 'rational/economic' point of view. This is clearly no longer enough: if it were enough, the present levels of technology and business development would deliver totally reliable products and services, to high and perfect standards, for the good of all (see Box 3.1).

> **Box 3.1 The Rational/Economic Perspective on Business and Management**
>
> The rational/economic view of business and management demands perfect markets, in which products and services are made available, produced, sold and delivered, on exactly the same basis to all. This view additionally asserts that given any choice, customers choose the lowest price for the greatest amount of goods and services. Prices will be brought down to equilibrium by perfect competition, and everyone in the market will act in the same ways at all times.
>
> In practice, of course, this is nonsense. There is no scientific basis in any rationale that says that 'a rational choice' is always the lowest cost. For any cost and charge for any product or service, there are always trade-offs between the stated charges and price, and utility, durability, quality,

> convenience (of purchase), speed of delivery, and where appropriate, ease of access to maintenance and upgrades and, when the time comes, ease of replacement. There are also always trade-offs between what is available and personal preference.
>
> It is therefore clear that people do not make rational choices; they make personal choices. It is therefore essential to turn the whole perspective on its head, and try and establish the true basis and bases for business and management effectiveness.

If the complexities indicated in Box 3.1 are to be understood, then the discipline and expertise required in order to manage companies and organisations in the fourth industrial revolution have to be enlarged and developed to accommodate this. The disciplines required relate to the socially and behaviourally driven keys of choice, utility, convenience, quality—and to the personal elements that go into defining them; and these personal elements, traits and preferences are founded in:

- sociology, in which people will seek to make choices based on belonging and conformity, and to be known within their circles as being 'good people';
- psychology, in which people make choices that develops and reinforces their own perceptions of worth, self-worth, self-respect and self-esteem; and the worth, respect and esteem of others whose opinions they value, and with whom they wish to identify and be identified with;
- anthropology, in which choices are influenced and driven, and reflected, by what society as a whole expects people of high self-value and self-worth are expected to make; and this is reinforced by media and other coverage and publicity and presentation. There are also wider issues of self-presentation in relation to society and its real and perceived social norms and values, that drive choices;
- ethics, in which people are seen to be 'doing the right things' in making their choices. Some ethical issues are absolute (e.g. right and wrong). Some ethical issues are current and transient (e.g. use of plastics; consumption of fossil fuels). In both cases, people's choices are influenced and driven by the prevailing ethical pressures.

There is also clearly a financial foundation also; however this must be understood in the broader and more detailed context set out above. The immediate conclusion is that people are disposed to pay more (not less) for products, services and recognition that enhance their wider standing and perceptions of self-respect and the respect and value of others. Other conclusions that may be drawn are as follows:

- products and services have to reflect each of the above in some way if they are to deliver the value that is sought, and for which people are actually prepared to pay;
- there is therefore an economic rent (i.e. the opportunity to charge more, not less), if products and services are known, believed or perceived to meet certain ethical standards, or trigger psychological cues, or identify with particular social norms.

It is also self-evidently true that low prices do not of themselves deliver value: value has to be present in every product or service. So for example:

- SouthWestern, Ryanair, easyJet and Wizz are all low-cost airlines that deliver full route networks that reflect the demands of their customers. The value lies in both the low charges and also the route network, not one or the other;
- Charity shops offering low-cost second-hand clothing do not make as many sales as department stores and clothing chains, and this is because customers of charity shops are not certain of the quality or value being delivered;
- There are supermarkets and chains and grocery products at all levels of price and value spectrum: if people were making purely economic choices the only companies that would survive in this sector would be those which offered the lowest prices.

The Relationships Between Business and Society

Business and businesses provide the infrastructure for every aspect of economic, social and human life. Every human activity is underpinned by the infrastructure that business provides. On the one hand, every activity is ultimately conducted on a 'business-like' basis; on the other hand, every economically driven transaction has to have measures of social delivery, and wider humanity, if they are to deliver value and economic and financial returns in some way (see Box 3.2).

> **Box 3.2 Miss-Selling Financial Services Products**
>
> One of the main financial scandals of the recent past has been the miss selling of financial services products. The staff of banks, insurance companies and financial services agencies were incentivised (and in many cases, openly pressurised and bullied) into selling high interest rate deposit accounts, personal protection insurance, payment insurances and credit card packages that customers either did not want or need, or else could not actually afford, or else had no actual value when the time came to either claim on them or redeem them. Among the worst examples were:
>
> - payment protection insurances that were described as giving full indemnity against major financial commitments (especially mortgage payments) and which turned out only to do this for up to 3–6 months if claims were ever made;
> - deposit accounts that risked capital as well as interest rate returns if the funds to which they were attached either underperformed or else failed in some other way;
> - personal pension plans that delivered only a fraction of the results promised;
> - credit card insurance which was completely unnecessary (as all Visa and MasterCard cards are protected by the main terms of usage);
> - high interest rate (subprime) mortgages and other loans to those least able to afford the repayments.
>
> These activities were founded purely in developing the economic and financial returns and accruals to the banks, finance and insurance companies and their staff. The error was compounded by the fact that the staff who actually sold the products gained very little in the way of incentive payments and bonuses; though they were liable to punishments, sanctions, discipline and in some cases dismissal, if they failed to try and sell these products.
>
> The result was that in the short term, the banks and finance companies made a lot of money. In the longer term, however, and as people began to realise the futility of the products that they had purchased, the companies found themselves having to meet an extensive range of liabilities.

> At first they set out to settle each case on an individual basis. Indeed many companies openly blamed 'rogue staff' for over selling and miss selling, rather than accepting overall responsibility and accountability.
>
> However, it very quickly became apparent that the issue was institutional rather than individual. It also very quickly became known and understood that every bank and finance company was involved. Accordingly, the whole sector was forced to underwrite itself and take active steps to ensure that everyone who had been miss sold (defrauded) got their money back.
>
> Had the companies involved ever looked at the issue from a human point of view, and delivered the products based on value and reliability (i.e. that the products would deliver what they promised to deliver), none of these issues would ever have occurred.
>
> Above all, top and senior directors, managers and executives would have looked elsewhere for profitable opportunities. They would additionally and crucially have looked at the humanity of what they were doing. They would have evaluated what the products delivered as well as the upfront charges and costs and revenues that they were generating; and so would have recognised and learned two critical lessons:
>
> - the economic nostrum that profit maximisation is the overall goal is false and must not therefore be a de facto a company objective (long-term profit optimisation is the true objective);
> - anyone or any organisation that behaves like this will eventually be called to account for it, and will have to make reparations.
>
> *Source* British Banking Association (2019)

INDUSTRY AND COMMERCE AS SOCIAL INFRASTRUCTURE

There is a central tenet in theories of economic development that state that production functions are located close to the markets if the products gain weight during production; and that production functions are located close to the source of raw materials if they lose weight during production processes. This is no longer (completely) true.

Socio-economic activity is now developed to the extent that products and services are delivered everywhere in the world, wherever they are produced. Transport networks are now much more fully developed. Instead of having to rely on pre-set delivery schedules, companies and organisations now have access to flexible, responsive and far reaching and well developed transport and communications and delivery networks, meaning that they can work with anyone anywhere in the world if they so choose. They can also develop their supply sides and materials, technology and expertise sourcing from wherever they choose.

The supply and distribution networks are all underpinned by more or less universal availability of technology and IT infrastructure. This means in turn that every new location for one activity can readily be evaluated for other opportunities at any time. It is necessary only to have the leadership and managerial expertise and acumen to recognise particular potential, and make a substantial case for developing it.

However, this availability additionally requires social evaluation in all cases. Again companies that have gone into particular locations on a purely economic basis have almost invariably either failed outright, or else have failed to deliver the high levels of profits that they had originally projected. Business ventures in any part of the world have to have social as well as economic fit. There has to be a cultural fit and empathy. Companies have to be comfortable in terms of their locations for their own confidence and collective wellbeing. Staff in particular locations have to be comfortable and assured on an individual as well as collective basis, in terms of being happy and settled in working for the particular company. Working people have to be assured that their families will enjoy a good quality of life. Health and education facilities have to be present, as well as the means of social engagement. From a social point of view, therefore, the particular location needs to be as assured and comfortable as possible about having the company present and working there, and delivering the wider social, business and economic development that are brought about as the result.

Conclusions

The key to successful business operations and activities is social assurance. Whatever the work provided and salaries paid, people have to be comfortable and assured from a human point of view, from the point of view of working in the organisation and of living in the society and location.

Leaders and managers need to know and understand that this comfort and assurance is founded in the transport, social and public services provisions in the given location; and as above this is built on in the first instance by having the confidence to have a family and social life there, as well as working. Organisations may attract people to specific locations with the promises of high salaries and challenging and rewarding work; however they will only keep their people if the other factors are in place.

Leaders and managers therefore in turn need to know and understand that everything has to be supported by the quality of life that is sought on both individual and also collective bases. The key issues to address therefore are:

- the need to have access to banks, shops, restaurants, bars, clubs, and sports and leisure facilities;
- the need for IT and web/internet access for personal as well as professional and occupational use;
- the need for social security supported by public services relating to family, collective and individual health and wellbeing;
- the need for social safety, underpinned by systems of policing, justice, recourse to law and personal assurance;
- the need to be able to both move into the area and also move away from the area, as required.

This part of management knowledge must therefore be developed. Leaders and managers who develop and establish business ventures, new markets and locations have an enduring responsibility for their staff in social as well as economic terms. This is driven by finance and economics as well as social considerations; companies that ignore this find themselves having to spend inordinate amounts of time, money and other resources on managing staff dissatisfaction, rather than attending to business drives and performance.

Managers need to know and understand that staff must be able to afford to carry out the work, in both economic and social terms. Again there is no point in offering fulfilling and rewarding and challenging work if the salaries on offer are not high enough to support a good quality of life in and away from work, or if the quality of life in the location is not adequate.

The position and expertise of leaders and leadership have to be developed to ensure that the behavioural and technology-driven approach to organisation strategy and operations is fully understood. This enhances decision-making, as well as contributing to the all-round strength of the organisation, from all of the points of view noted above. It is essential also that leaders, and top and senior managers and executives know and understand the consequences of not attending to these matters.

REFERENCES AND FURTHER READING

Briody, E., R. Trotter, and T. Meerwarth. 2010. *Transforming Culture*. Palgrave Macmillan.
British Bankers Association. 2019. *Digital Disruption*. BBA Publications.
Davis, P., and L.-Y. Roy. 2019. *Simulating Societal Change: Counterfactual Modelling for Social and Policy Inquiry*. Springer.
Drucker, P.F. 1998. *The Effective Executive*. Routledge.
Glatzer, W., L. Camfield, V. Møller, and M. Rojas (eds.). 2015. *Global Handbook of Quality of Life: Exploration of Well-Being of Nations and Continents*. Free Press.
Pettinger, R. 2011. *Organisational Behaviour*. Routledge.
Tonon, G. 2020. *Teaching Quality of Life in Different Domains*. Springer.

CHAPTER 4

The Disciplines of Business

Abstract The main disciplines of business are introduced: strategy; marketing; finance; product and service delivery; and staffing. These disciplines are evaluated from a social and economic point of view. The influences of technology and the new and evolving organisation forms are noted, and the work opportunities and constraints that are delivered as the result. This chapter also refers to the need to deliver human and social value as a condition of effective business.

Keywords Disciplines of business · Strategy · Core strategy · Staffing · Niches · Production and service delivery · Cost and finance · Working environment · Markets and marketing

INTRODUCTION

In recent years the relationships between business and society have come under much greater scrutiny; and this has been driven into very sharp focus by the COVID19 pandemic of 2020 and beyond. The initial positions are therefore:

- business exists to serve the interests of society as a whole, and the individuals who make up that society;
- society provides the demands, needs and wants that business and businesses have to fulfil;
- the strength of society depends on the volume, quality and effectiveness of the contribution that everybody makes;
- at some point, everyone will make demands on society and therefore business and businesses; and at some point, everyone will deliver to the demands, needs and wants of society.

The nature of business and businesses is therefore a direct function of these demands, needs and wants. Rationally, needs are very few: food, drink, water, energy and shelter. However, business and businesses provide additional social and behavioural needs (and these are needs) as follows:

- individual and collective needs for achievement, recognition and esteem;
- individual and collective needs for delivering self-worth and self-respect, and the respect of others;
- individual and collective needs for social as well as occupational belonging and interactions;
- individual and collective needs for friends, colleagues, belonging and contribution;
- individual and collective needs for comfort and wellbeing.

Because people spend so much time at work, they need to gain responses to all of these needs from work as well as non-work living. People therefore tend to choose to work with others whom they like and respect, who share the same values and aspirations, and the same levels of respect for both each other and for society at large.

At present, therefore, there is a critical drive to understand the overall relationship between business and organisations and society. It is therefore necessary to evaluate the disciplines of business from a social and behavioural point of view.

Strategy

Business strategy has existed as a separate discipline for over fifty years; and in many cases in the historic past, strategy has been developed from a behavioural point of view, with very great and enduring success. For example:

- Cadbury, the chocolate company, and the Lever brothers, the washing powder and detergent company, built good quality homes and communities for their workers. They also ensured that their workers were well fed, educated and provided with such health care as was available at the time. This was to ensure that they always got good and assured production from healthy workforces of course; however they also understood that this was only possible if people were fundamentally settled socially.
- John Lewis founded what is now the John Lewis Partnership and the Waitrose supermarket chain on the basis that everyone was a partner. Everyone who works for the partnership therefore got (and gets) a share that entitles them to benefits in cash and kind, and to be a part of a wider and community-led approach to work and occupation.
- Nissan, the Japanese car manufacturer, committed to spend £3000 per employee on training and development each year. This was (and is) not optional; people have to take this benefit and use it. Nissan also runs a very extensive occupational and personal health programme, which has the twin purposes of ensuring that everyone turns up to work and then works as directed; and that if they do have medical conditions or illnesses, they will be well looked after.

Many other companies and organisations have adopted similar approaches. The reasoning is that any company strategy is only effective if it can be executed and delivered; and that this is only possible if everyone is present and healthy and able while they are at work.

This is not altruism or undisciplined. It is a fundamental commitment made by the organisations in terms of their wage—work bargain; and it is a wider commitment to the employment contract and identity with the place of work (the psychological contract). If people have this kind of identity and engagement, there is a much better chance of people committing to organisation purpose and activities.

Core and Foundation Strategies

The Porter (1980, 1985) view of strategy is that there are three fundamental generic strategic positions:

- cost leadership and cost advantage, in which everything is driven by seeking to become the lowest cost operator in the field.
- brand leadership, brand advantage and differentiation, in which everything is driven by seeking to be the highest value operator in the field.
- niche and specialisation, in which everything is driven by the need to be able to deliver everything that a client or customer base needs or wants from a particular specialist.

From a behavioural as well as economic point of view the assertions made by Porter remain valid. However, the view needs to be developed as follows.

The drive for cost leadership and advantage is a function of delivering financial profit and surplus; and the levels of profit demanded are the result of human behaviour and judgement. People 'expect' certain levels of profit and financial performance; and those levels are again determined by human behaviour and judgement.

The drive for brand advantage requires that companies and organisations differentiate in ways that are socially acceptable. Branding delivers confidence, assurance and reassurance, as well as self-recognition and the recognition of others in purchases made.

Niches and specialisms are founded on personal as well as professional confidence; and this confidence is founded in liking and respect, as well as the assurance of professional competence and worth.

Indeed, in many cases the nature of cost is not fully evaluated from a behavioural point of view. The fact that you can produce items at low cost does not mean that you have to sell them at low cost. On many items produced at low cost the sale price is very high (e.g. cosmetics and electrical goods); and this is the result of branding and differentiation.

On many items people expect to pay a particular price; and if the price is too low, they will not buy as they do not value the item. This 'value' is also driven by human perception and behaviour: the prices charged do not reflect self-worth or self-esteem. Or else people go to the upper ends of product ranges for the (real and perceived) assurance of product and service performance that high prices (are supposed to) deliver. The value is then reflected in the self-respect that comes from owning and using high priced products and services.

Markets

It is a critical point that if the only thing that drove markets was cost, then everyone would buy the lowest cost option. There is a widespread business and management myth that low cost/price is the 'rational' choice that consumers and customers and clients will always make. This is simply not true:

- the best selling mobile devices are made by Apple and Samsung, and these are the most expensive;
- the best selling cola drinks are Coca Cola and Pepsi Cola and these are the most expensive;
- mass consumer markets are serviced by branded goods, mainly of mid-range prices; the best selling toothpaste and detergents are branded goods made by mass manufacturers (e.g. Colgate, Unilever);
- where a real or perceived low-cost situation has been developed, the assurance of worth (the human response) has to be in place. The route networks of Ryanair, Wizz and Southwestern have no value unless the service itself is assured, however low the ticket prices.

Niches

People who operate in niche and specialist markets are expected by their customers and clients to deliver everything that the particular specialism demands. Companies and individuals who buy in specialist services are prepared to pay very high prices for the reassurance of worth and confidence that the high prices (are supposed to) guarantee. These high levels are reinforced in many cases by assurances of speed of response, completeness of service and other add ons that all compose the overall relationship.

Each of these elements is a human drive. The demands for speed, completeness and assurance of products, services and above all service, transcend business demands. Additionally, as these relationships develop, both buyers and sellers develop a mutual human as well as professional confidence. As they become satisfied with the working relationship, a human relationship develops also, and in these situations those involved find themselves looking forward to the next interaction and pieces of work.

Those who work in niches also have to develop their own expertise, as the demands of the customers and clients change. This reinforces the human value that work delivers. If expertise was assured and limited, people would move on once their work had been delivered, and would be replaced by someone else. This happens in some cases; in many others, people develop as they grow the work and grow into the work.

This is rewarding from a human as well as occupational point of view. It adds to the overall purpose of making organisations effective as human as well as occupational places; both as people and as job holders, everyone needs to recognise and mark their own progress. Indeed people will leave organisations if they have any choice in the matter, if they are not allowed to progress and grow; and this applies to everyone, whatever their job or occupation or social standing.

Marketing

Marketing is increasingly becoming one of the most scientific parts of business practice and expertise. From its roots in creativity and design and presentation, marketing is growing into a data driven and much more precise range of activities. This is because there is now so much data available to companies and organisations about human behaviour and choice; and because the capacity now exists to analyse and evaluate consumer behaviour from the data in terms of what they **will** buy, use and consume; and not just what they **might** or **would** buy, use and consume.

Staffing

Present and recent developments in relation to the organisation of work have meant that a much greater flexibility and operationally driven approach to work structures and job content are possible. IT and the technology infrastructure mean that a lot of work that has traditionally been done in offices can now be done from anywhere: hotel suites; flexible work locations; home; and on travels. This brings advantages and pitfalls as follows.

The advantages are the ability to employ people, and for people to work, at times and locations that are suitable to them, provided that the key deliverables of the jobs and tasks can be achieved. It removes travel to work time and the expense and stress of having to get into the office or computer suite. It removes the pressures on transport networks and other parts of the infrastructure. Connectivity through meeting technology and platforms means that people from anywhere in the world can if necessary be called together at very short notice, rather than having to wait for travel arrangements.

There are pitfalls however. Home locations have to be fully and properly equipped and insured. Risk assessments are required, in terms of time spent on screen and the nature of equipment and technology provided. Risk assessments are also required in relation to isolation and alienation. Risk assessments are required in terms of technology assurance, connectivity and security.

Home locations have to be physically large enough to be capable of use as a work station; and this means attention to domestic and non-work life, and this aspect of the work/life balance. People have to have the active means of replacing the social as well as professional/occupational infrastructure to which they have become used. Feelings of isolation and alienation can and do emerge. People who work in these ways have to be capable of self-motivation; and in many cases this means having to set out a schedule that would otherwise be provided as the result of attending a place of work.

This also applies to using flexible locations. People have to be supported in their use of flexible locations, in terms of security, assurance of connectivity, expenses incurred and other aspects of working from the car/train/airport, and from bespoke business centres.

There is therefore a critical behavioural input that is required by organisations that work in these ways, and that requires staff to work in these ways. A key part of the changing nature of staffing and HR practice is the ability to on-board, embed and provide social as well as occupational structures for staff who work remotely and flexibly. This requires investment and commitment, and attention to these key aspects of operations and behaviour. There are clearly cost savings to be made, and efficiencies to be gained; however the new ways of working have to be substantially underpinned and invested in, if they are to be effective—and profitable.

Production and Service Delivery

Over the past fifty years, production of goods has undergone a revolution in terms of:

- the ability to make products that are enduringly reliable and assured;
- from mass employment to mass automation;
- ever greater attention to absolute quality and uniformity of components and finished products;
- the ability to make to order through using just in time production and sourcing techniques;
- the ability to make short and flexible run batches of products through the use of core and flexible production technologies;
- attention to the supply chains to ensure that components and raw materials are delivered more frequently thus removing needs for large storage areas and stockpiling (which in many cases used to mean that components became obsolete before they were used and so had to be discarded).

This in turn has changed the core manufacturing occupations in human terms, from being 'unskilled' and manual, to machine operations. Many such occupations are now driven by extensive robotic and machine managing training and development, and full flexibility of working.

Services delivery has also transformed. This as above is partly as the result of being able to locate service delivery people in the communities where they work, as opposed to having them operating from central organisation locations. Those who work in some public services (e.g. community health and social care) can also do this from home or other flexible and convenient locations within their communities. This has led again to working advantages and concerns around isolation and real and perceived lack of support. It has also led to what is called 'the gig economy' and zero hours contracts, and in many cases very oppressive service level contracts and agreements that are very difficult to follow in the context of busy roads and traffic hold ups.

Again however, the services depend on making attractive the ways of working to those who have the qualities and expertise to deliver them when and where they are required. This In turn requires that the people carrying out the services are fully and adequately rewarded. They need also to have absolute assurance that the telecoms and IT structures and the technology that supports them are reliable and secure at all times. This is a part of the organisation commitment to getting its services delivered; and failure to do this means that organisations will lose staff to those who do take more care of their people, whatever the organisation structure may be.

Conclusions

The chapter has concentrated on reviewing the disciplines of business from the perspective of managing behaviour in the present and unfolding socio-economic situation and climate. It identifies the shift from physical presence to changed patterns of work and especially remote working as being made effective through attention to behaviour and technology, rather than costs and finance.

Costs and finance are nevertheless central to the overall effectiveness of anything that any organisation ever does. In this context, premises costs are likely to be reduced as the demands for space diminishes; or else premises are likely to be shifted to primary organisation purposes of product and service design, production and delivery activities. This means that the key and more or less universal organisation drive for maximum and optimum cost-effectiveness and efficiency is attended to and delivered. It is clear also that a proportion of the savings will have to be reinvested in ensuring that those who do work remotely are as fully resourced and supported as they would otherwise be at a place of work.

Additionally, it is essential to recognise that many activities still require attendance at a place of work. This applies to both production and also services delivery. Much greater attention is required to ensuring a safe and above all healthy working environment; and for the foreseeable future this means paying attention especially to whatever social spacing requirements are deemed necessary.

This in turn requires a shift of both emphasis and also expertise. Leaders and managers are not used to thinking of things in these ways. Yet it is a key feature of the expertise that is required if organisations are going to be as fully and enduringly as effective as possible. Changes in organisation and social structures require changes in how leadership is exercised so that all of the disciplines of business, which are essential for organisation survival and effectiveness, remain strong and substantial.

References and Further Reading

Boyatzis, R., M. Smith, and E. Van Osten. 2019. *Helping People Change*. Harvard.
Goleman, D. 1995. *Emotional Intelligence*. Bantam.
Grattan, L. 2005. *Living Strategy*. Pearson.
Peters, T., and N. Austin. 1988. *Thriving on Chaos*. Harper and Row.
Pettinger, R. 2005. *Contemporary Strategic Management*. Palgrave.
Porter, M.E. 1980. *Competitive Strategy*. Free Press.
Porter, M.E. 1985. *The Competitive Advantage of Nations*. Free Press.
Yeung, A., and D. Ulrich. 2019. *Reinventing the Organisation*. Harvard.

CHAPTER 5

The Economic Environment

Abstract This chapter evaluates the environment from a far more detailed perspective than is usual. It especially draws attention to the social and behavioural issues that have to be considered. There is a far more detailed method proposed for addressing and classifying the different environmental factors that are of value to society as well as delivering the economic demands necessary.

Keywords Organisations · Organisation purpose · Economic environment · Competition · Open and closed economies · Analysing the environment · Socio-technological approach

INTRODUCTION

An organisation is any entity or body that is constituted for a given purpose, and which then establishes and conducts activities in pursuit of this purpose. Leaders, directors and managers are then employed by the owners and directors of organisations to run them on their behalf.

Organisations are created on the basis that more can be achieved by people working in harmony and towards a stated purpose than by individuals acting alone. It is also more efficient and effective to specialise, at least to some extent, in seeking to serve or fulfil a given set of wants or needs. Resources, technology, expertise, information, finance and property can then be commanded and ordered for the stated purpose, within the constraints of the environment.

The result of this is that society and the economy are more or less founded on a highly complex network of organisations, each of which serves a given purpose and all of which serve the entire range of purposes required. Organisations pervade all aspects of life—economic, social, political, cultural, religious, communal and family. They serve needs and essentials—food, shelter, health, IT, energy, education, water, energy, transport and communications; as well as wants and choices—cola, cinema, football. They serve what are understood to be 'public services': services including health and social care, policing and security, overall infrastructure maintenance and development.

Other organisations are constituted to deliver the social, political and economic infrastructure. There are therefore political, legal/judiciary, economic, security, military and other organisations. These organisations are staffed by people who have the skills and expertise to deliver these activities and functions, which provide a fundamental governance to the society as a whole, and the ways in which it functions.

Society and its different groups also require that organisations deliver 'not for profit' activities: and so there are such organisations as: charities; specialist and advisory bodies; regulatory and public health and safety standards; and other key social, political and economic activities.

Organisations provide employment for all, and consequently underpin the patterns of life that everyone follows. For those who work in them, organisations form a distinctive and significant of their part of, and participation in, society.

Human beings generally need, want and enjoy the company of other people. Business and work organisations therefore fulfil social as well as technical, technological, occupational and professional needs, as well as delivering on the key economic demands of producing, delivering and supplying products, services, needs and wants.

There is therefore a great complexity in the relationships between, and within, organisations, organisations and their place in the wider environment; between those who work within them; and between organisations and those who come to them from products and services. There is also the critical influence that every organisation and its activities has on collective and individual behaviour; and this part of environmental analysis ought to be a key influence on managerial knowledge and expertise.

This chapter draws on and develops standard and well known analytical approaches to the organisational and operating environment. It specifically reviews and develops the PESTEL approach to give a much greater emphasis to behavioural, social and technological factors.

THE ECONOMIC ENVIRONMENT

The economic environment is the core of the context in which all business, managerial and organisational activities take place. Of key concern are the following:

- the overall structure of the economic environment, and the mix of commercial, public service and not for profit activities that are conducted;
- the potential for growth and opportunities;
- the volumes and value of business conducted;
- key macro issues including: money supply; interest and inflation rates;
- the rates of business growth, both overall and also by sector and location;
- employment rates and density; and unemployment rates and whether unemployment is structural or transitional;
- pay, wage and salary rates, and the resultant propensities to spend and save;
- the frequency, value and volumes of business transactions, both overall and also by sector, location and activity;
- the structure and quality of the business infrastructure, including: transport; access and egress; telecommunications; physical and technological/virtual connectivity; IT systems and other technology; and commercial and domestic property;
- availability of skilled staff with required and demanded expertise;
- 'market rates' for specific skills and expertise;
- specific actions taken by national, regional and local government to develop and 'pump prime' activities, by sector, location and activities;

- other impacts and interventions by national, regional and local government and their agencies (e.g. training schemes; regeneration schemes; support for particular activities where there are shortages).

In specific locations, it is necessary to be aware of and evaluate the impacts of key industries, dominant employers and occupations, in terms of setting wage, salary and pay rates that are both competitive overall, and also of value to prospective staff.

It is essential to recognise that no part of any economy stands still. Even if the economy is not growing in financial and monetary values, organisations and their staff are constantly looking to improve, to try out new things, to get more value from existing capacities and to reduce critical factors such as wastage and staff turnover.

It is also essential to recognise that the economic environment is competitive. All organisations compete for business, resources, technology, markets and profits. All organisations also compete for a share of the disposable income of customers, clients and consumers; and this competition takes place at a range of different levels (see Box 5.1).

Box 5.1 Competition at Different Levels

Understanding how companies compete at different levels requires understanding the key complexities of competition as follows.

Macro and organisational level: e.g. Coca Cola and Pepsi Cola; McDonalds and Burger King; Starbucks and Costa

Locality level: in which there is competition for local customers according to which companies and organisations are serving specific needs (e.g. as well as competition in a locality between Starbucks and Costa, there are likely to be niche and specialist brands, local and independent providers)

Competition for customer spend: e.g. if customers have limited funds and can choose either a burger or the fare home, then the food outlet and the transport company are in competition at that moment.

Collaborations: of which the following are examples:

- joint ventures to enable companies to take on work and markets that they would not otherwise be able to enter;

> - price fixing and cartel: where all companies in a market agree to charge similar prices for their work;
> - where one company sells the products of others (a major contribution to the food retail sector);
> - where one company underwrites the efforts of others (e.g. branded insurance products sold by brokers);
> - where one company gains work and then subcontracts it to another company.
>
> **Alternatives**: where companies do not directly compete, but where one company offers an equivalent and/or alternative to what is already available. Examples are:
>
> - Ryanair which competes directly on very few routes, providing an equivalent or near equivalent alternative from and/or to particular destinations relative to high-value flag carrier airlines (e.g. London Stansted—Paris Beauvais, rather than London Heathrow—Paris Charles de Gaulle);
> - Aldi and Lidl which offer a clear alternative range of groceries to other UK and European supermarkets;
> - Airbnb, which offers alternative accommodation for travellers, rather than directly competing with branded hotels.

It is usual to define economies and economic systems as being either open or closed. The open system accepts that individual organisations will act independently of external concerns or pressures. Resources are taken as required from the supply side, and are used and consumed in producing outputs, products and services. Pollution, waste and effluent are 'natural' parts of production processes; and the waste and effluents are then passed on to specialist companies to be disposed of. The management of waste and pollutants becomes an additional business opportunity, crucial to the effective overall quality of life in a particular society (see Fig. 5.1).

In the closed economy, a much broader view is taken of resource usage. The need to make and deliver products and services is just as central. The closed economy recognises the potential to reuse and recycle obsolete products especially, turning then into goods for new markets and future generations of consumers and end users. Much closer attention is also paid to the amounts of pollution, waste and effluent generated.

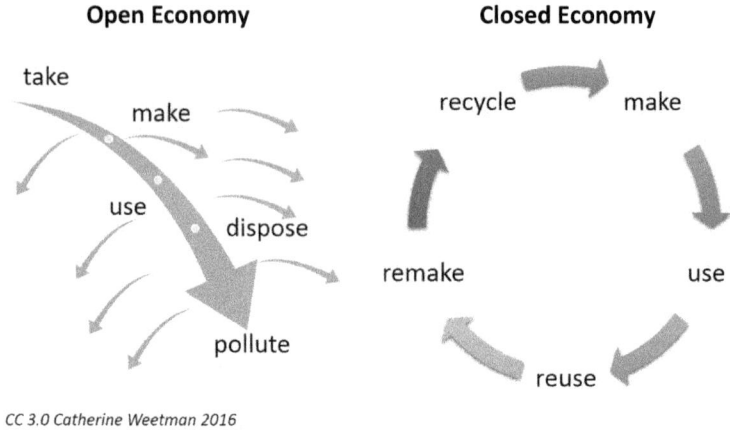

CC 3.0 Catherine Weetman 2016

Fig. 5.1 Open and closed economies

Companies and organisations in closed economies pay much more attention to non-reusable resources, especially fuel and energy. In prosperous times, fuel and energy prices tend to rise because of increasing collective demand. When times are less prosperous, companies and organisations pay attention to costs that can be managed, including fuel and energy. In the COVID19 pandemic of 2020 and beyond, when energy prices fell sharply due to a major drop in overall demand, companies and organisations nevertheless took the opportunity to reposition their energy usage while on lockdown, restrictions on the conduct of business, and other constraints.

In closed economies, there are nevertheless specific external inputs required in order to make them function effectively. There will always be demands for raw materials and energy, though reduced relative to open economies. New technology is bought in as required. IT, communications and streaming systems and services have also to be bought in and installed (and then disposed of when they are truly obsolete).

Closed economies work within either specific communities or localities. The hypothesis is that within a given community, everyone has a role and part to play in delivering the economic returns required; and to do this means that everyone accepts that they have a part to play in serving the common good as well as their own individual interests, needs and wants. Porter (1998) noted this as clustering: the process of ensuring that every locality or 'cluster' could be self-sufficient, subject only to the need to bring in essential supplies (including expertise as well as raw materials).

However, the concept of closed economies may be seen to inform all organisations of the value of using resources as efficiently as possible, and to take advantage of whatever savings and efficiencies can be achieved. Again this is especially vital in the COVID19 and post COVID19 world, where maximising (rather than optimising) resource usage is certain to be a much greater leadership and management priority.

The other key economic deliverable of the COVID19 crisis is a fresh evaluation of what are deemed to be 'essential' industries. These are the industries, services and provisions that need to be available in all locations. At the onset of the COVID19 pandemic it quickly became clear that 'essential' workers included: van and truck drivers; retail staff; postal and other communications staff; refuse management and disposal; as well as health and social care staff. Additionally, a critical lesson was also to ensure that there would always be immediate (and when required) urgent access to a comprehensive range of medicines, pharmaceuticals, protective clothing and equipment, as well as assurances of food and fuel supplies, and access to technology and IT systems.

In the period up until early 2020, the received wisdom was that everything could be supplied on regularised and assured global and international supply chains, using the 'best' sources anywhere in the world. During the crisis it became clear that many of these essential items were not readily available. There were delays in getting even the most basic of these products either quickly enough or in the required volumes. The use of local resources, even if this means a higher cost and price, to ensure that such items are available when required is a further critical shift; and it may mean that such items are produced within closed rather than open economies.

Analysing the Environment

Environmental analyses are conducted to ensure that each aspect of the organisation, and its competitive and general environment, and the pressures present, are clearly understood. The approaches used are as follows.

- SWOT analysis, which identifies and classifies the external, internal and competitive forces present under the headings of: strengths; weaknesses; opportunities; and threats;
- PESTEL analysis, which identifies and classifies the forces present under the headings of: political; economic; social; technological; environmental/ethical; and legal;
- five forces analysis, which classifies the forces present under the headings of: rivalry with other companies; power of customers and consumers; power of suppliers; threats of entry to the market by potential incomers; threats of substitution of other and new products and services.

The purpose of analysing the environment is to be able to identify, separate out and classify the forces present. These forces are then evaluated and prioritised in terms of their impact on the organisation, and the opportunities and constraints placed on organisational and managerial activities and priorities.

A Socio-Technological View of Business and Environment Analyses

SWOT, PESTEL and five forces analyses deliver a body of agreed knowledge and understanding that ought to be of value to all managers. For the specific purposes of developing the discipline of analysing the environment in full, and to ensure the maximum completeness of coverage, the data produced by environmental analyses can be developed in more detail.

A key approach is to break down the SWOT and PESTEL still further. Cartwright (2001) proposed a more detailed approach, using the acronym SPECTACLES, as follows:

- **Social**: changes in society and societal trends; demographic trends and influences; population movements and relocations; industrial and commercial reorganisation and development;
- **Political**: political processes and structures; lobbying; national and international political institutions; the political pressures brought about as the result of key national and international regulations, agreements and treaties;

- **Economic**: referring especially to sources of finance; stock markets; inflation; interest rates; government and international economic policy; local, regional, national and global economies;
- **Cultural**: international and national cultures; regional cultures; local cultures; organisational cultures; cultural clashes; culture changes; cultural pressures on business and organisational activities; changes in patterns of work; specific attention to quality of life and quality of working life;
- **Technological**: understanding the technological needs of business; technological pressures; the relationship between technology and work patterns; the need to invest in technology; communications; current developments and their potential; e-commerce; technology and manufacturing; technology and biochemistry and bioengineering; technological potential; technology development as a continuous process;
- **Aesthetic**: organisation and product and service design and appearance; the nature of communications; marketing and promotion; image; fashion; organisational body language; public relations; use of media; organisation projection and presentation;
- **Customer**: consumerism; the importance of analysing the data available from customer and client bases; customer needs and wants; customer care; anticipating future customer requirements; customer behaviour;
- **Legal**: the impact of legal constraints; specific codes of practice; legal pressures; product liability; service liability; health and safety; employment law; competition legislation; safety and security legislation; national and international legal pressures; and whistle blowing;
- **Environmental/ethical**: responsibilities to the planet; responsibilities to communities; pollution; waste management; cost–benefit analyses; legal and social pressures;
- **Sectoral**: competition; cartels, monopolies and oligopolies; competitive forces; cooperation within sectors; differentiation; and segmentation.

The SPECTACLES approach provides very much more detail in everything that is identified, classified and prioritised. It deepens and widens the scope of analysis that needs to be carried out in order to include a more detailed consideration of the environment, society and culture within which an organisation must operate. This approach requires managers to take a much more detailed look at every aspect of their operations within their particular environment and sphere of activities. It also emphasises the detailed attention required to the cataclysmic changes brought about by the COVID19 pandemic.

Conclusions

The key purpose of adopting a socio-technological approach to knowing and understanding the economy and the environment of business is therefore to identify and develop overall organisational and managerial knowledge and understanding of the ways in which the economy truly operates. This in turn is a core part of the expertise of knowing and understanding the full complexities of the economic environment; and knowing and understanding this is the fullest possible detail is essential.

Leaders and managers—and entrepreneurs—need social as well as economic expertise if they are to understand where the drives and pressures come from, and where opportunities are genuinely likely to lie. They need to know what is of importance and value to the society and its members, in order to be able to develop business and contributory activities, products and services that will then in turn deliver profit.

A technological perspective is essential also, in that all economic activities, and the organisations within the economy, depend to a greater or lesser extent on technology in all its forms (see Chapter 2). All parts of society and societies now demand assured IT and communications technology as being key to developing and sustaining any kind of productive or service delivery activities. Without adequate access to technology and IT, there is very little chance of developing or sustaining any form of competitive activity.

Finally, there is nothing new about requiring that leaders and managers take the fullest possible view of the environment in which business is conducted; though they do need to develop this expertise as a consequence of the rapidly changing environment. Taking the widest and deepest perspective means that leaders and managers know how and why the economy and the business environment operate in particular ways. Having this range and depth of knowledge is therefore an essential informant of effective decision-making at all levels; and this in turn makes it a key part of management growth and development.

REFERENCES AND FURTHER READING

Braun, E. 2014. *Futile Progress: Technology's Empty Promise.* Earthscan.
Cartwright, R. 2001. *Mastering the Business Environment.* Palgrave Masters.
Dalio, R. 2019. *Principles for Success.* Simon and Schuster.
Pettinger, R. 2002. *Mastering the Skills of Management.* Palgrave Masters.
Porter, M.E. 1998. *Clusters and the New Economics of Competition* Harvard.
Weetman, C. 2016. *The Ellen Macarthur Foundation.* EMF Publications.

CHAPTER 6

Products and Services

Abstract This chapter evaluates the demands, needs and wants for products and services, as society evolves because of technological advances, and in terms also of what is truly vital and of value in the pandemic and post-pandemic world. Especially, the COVID19 crisis of 2020 and beyond is causing companies and organisations in all sectors to re-evaluate how they produce, deliver and service their products and services. This in turn informs what is developed, by whom and for whom. This has also led to demands and drives for some key products and services to be produced and delivered within specific localities, so that everyone who needs them has ready and easy access.

Keywords Products and services · Value · New product and service development · Service levels · Quality · Approaches to new product and services developments · Product and service appraisal and reappraisal

INTRODUCTION

There is an ever greater demand for products and services that serve the interests of everyone in a technology-driven society. Additionally, because of technology, supply and distribution chains can be created and sourced anywhere in the world. It is possible to get any product to anywhere in the world in two days; and so it is possible to obtain any product from anywhere in the world in two days also.

This is the attitude and approach that is driving so much business, product and service development. It follows from this that it is essential to recognise that competition and substitute and alternative products and services can be delivered in particular markets by companies and organisations located anywhere in the world also.

The COVID19 crisis of 2020 and beyond is causing companies and organisations in all sectors to re-evaluate how they produce, deliver and service their products and services. Supply, production and delivery processes are going to be ever more simplified and streamlined in order to keep resource utilisation to a minimum and in order to be able to meet changing patterns of consumption, which in turn are being brought on by a combination of poverty, self and social isolation, and the perceived convenience of having things delivered rather than collected.

It is also the case that the potential for developing products and services is every more enhanced by the availability of technology and different approaches to product and service manufacture, creation and delivery. The boom in cheap air travel in many parts of the world has caused those in many industries to take a fresh and original look at how their sectors do business, and whether there might be opportunities to disrupt in the same ways as the air travel boom has produced (see Box 6.1).

Box 6.1 Doing a Ryanair?

Before the boom in cheap air travel in Europe pioneered by Ryanair and easyJet, the European national and flag carrying airlines provided excellent service in return for very high fares and charges to a limited number of passengers.

When Ryanair then provided everything that the flag carriers delivered, but for a tiny fraction of the cost, the existing airlines went into denial. It was not possible or feasible for a private company to provide such services: every airline needed to carry a national brand by which it was identified.

As Ryanair, easyJet and subsequently others developed and grew, it quickly became apparent that there was a huge untapped market for air travel, provided that the prices, costs and charges could be kept down; and provided that the route network and flight schedules were assured and met quality, convenience and reliability standards.

This has caused many leaders and managers in a great variety of industries to re-evaluate their whole position, and how they should be able to operate. In many cases the starting point is the same as for the low-cost airlines: there is a huge demand for particular products and services, but not at the prices and costs charged by mainstream companies in particular sectors. For example:

- in the UK there is a huge demand for housing, but not at the very high land and building costs and charges; and this has led to growth in such diverse sectors as: trailer parks; self-assembly houses; prefabricated housing units and subunits;
- the costs and charges in car markets have led to an influx of low cost/high value products from companies such as Dacia and Hinari; and while these companies have only limited market shares, their position is growing all of the time. This has also led to existing and mainstream car companies developing separate brands for specific sectors (e.g. Volkswagen manufacture and deliver good value cars under the SEAT brand in order not to dilute the company's core brand and central products);
- the costs and prices charged for fast moving consumer goods (FMCG) has led to the development of companies such as Poundland, which now sell both mainstream and also alternative brands for a fraction of the prices charged elsewhere;
- high and rising levels of charges for proprietary and specialist pharmaceutical and healthcare products have caused others to look to low cost and mass market alternatives. To date this has covered aspirin and paracetamol (UK) and basic antibiotics (Spain); more are certain to follow;
- high and rising levels of food prices have led to the growth of lower cost/good value supermarket chains (e.g. Aldi; Lidl; Iceland)
- high and rising property prices over the whole of the first twenty years of the twenty-first century caused many in the building and construction industries to try and seek other ways of reducing construction costs for premises and housing.

All of these examples are informing leaders, entrepreneurs and managers in all sectors in terms of having them think and evaluate how their own businesses might develop; and also how their own businesses might be threatened, and where the source or sources of those threats might conceivably come from.

> This approach is certain to gather momentum as the world emerges from the COVID19 crisis of 2020 and beyond. Everyone will look to new and alternative ways of delivering products and services, and one key approach is to re-evaluate the levels of costs and charges and prices hitherto asked for, across all sectors.

PRODUCTS AND SERVICES

In practice there are very few completely new inventions. Pettinger (2019) defines genuine inventions as follows:

- The wheel;
- Reading, writing and mathematics;
- Harnessing electricity as energy and generating electric and nonelectric energy;
- Combining elements into products.

Everything that is done, every product that is made, every service that is delivered, is derived from one or more of these sources. The key issues are therefore founded in taking existing products and services and making them as fully effective as possible; and ensuring also that value is delivered at all times (however that value may be defined).

In terms of the post-COVID19 world, all aspects of value are to be redefined, as follows:

- What is of importance and value to consumers in a pandemic and post-pandemic world;
- Access to prioritised and non prioritised products and services;
- Costs and charges apportioned to products and services.

Value is also to be defined in terms of collective public confidence. However attractive particular products, services and events may be, people will not consume if they do not have the confidence to go to the locations or establishments that are providing the products and services.

It is clear in turn that the means of distribution is vital to ensuring continuing value. Companies such as Amazon that have more or less assured delivery systems are at present setting the standard for distribution; and others who wish to compete have to establish themselves to the same levels of confidence and assurance if value is to be made clear.

Value is also to be defined in terms of changing habits and priorities; and this will be influenced by new norms and levels of income post-pandemic.

There are some key and hitherto assured sectors which will have to reposition in terms of real and perceived value delivered. For these sectors, there are two key value propositions that have to be addressed:

- Real and perceived value to customers in terms of costs, benefits and convenience and utility;
- Real and perceived value in terms of resource usage, recycling and reuse capacity and potential.

At particular risk of losing value are clothing companies of all levels and quality, furniture stores, independent restaurants and bars, newspaper and magazine publishers, independent specialist boutique shops in all sectors, department stores, other physical retail chains and outlets.

Unless value is designed and determined in these ways, rather than assumed, many organisations will see themselves losing markets and market share. Companies and organisations in these and other sectors are also going to have to take a much broader view of their responsibilities for waste disposal and recycling; in these sectors neither has yet become a priority.

It follows from this that the definition of value is to be constantly addressed and revisited. There are some key industries that continue to shape, develop and influence the future, and this is because they produce goods and services that are either known, believed or perceived to be essential to the strength and viability of society and its infrastructure.

These industries and sectors include:

- Food and drink; other domestic products and services (e.g. for cleaning and washing);
- Transport and travel by road, rail, air and sea; and the cars, trucks, planes, ships and rolling stock that are used by each of these;
- Utilities: electricity, gas, water, roads, railways and IT and telecoms providers;

- Construction and civil and environmental engineering;
- Banking, finance and insurance and investment products and services;
- IT and telecoms networks and providers;
- Medicine and medical and healthcare products; pharmaceuticals and drugs; health technology and health and social care products and supports;
- Data management and analyses and informatics in all sectors.

There are some key industries which will become radically different to what they are now. These industries have to address and overcome the changes brought on by COVID19 and the IT revolution. They will need to develop radical new positions and approaches to their hitherto existing and largely assured customer bases.

Also at risk are the broadcasting, sports, leisure and travel and tourism sectors. In these sectors also, there are key social drives that have to be taken into account. Continued attention to social distancing, travel restrictions and virus management mean that hitherto assured volumes of business will not longer be present. New approaches and industrial and sectoral repositioning will see radical changes to these sectors.

There is therefore a complex context in which to see all new product and service developments Also see Chapter 5 above).

New Product and Service Developments

Given the position of waste and effluent management, and the need to gain maximum use from resources noted above, new product and service development cycles need to inbuild a fundamentally different approach to new product and service development (see Fig. 6.1).

The key issues of waste and effluent generation, resource and materials usage and reusage have to be included at the conception and brainstorming stages, as well as being evaluated as a core feature at the feasibility stage. A large part of the real and perceived value delivered by products and services is the presentation and packaging; and this is an issue to be addressed and managed as companies and organisations progress from the present situation and environment.

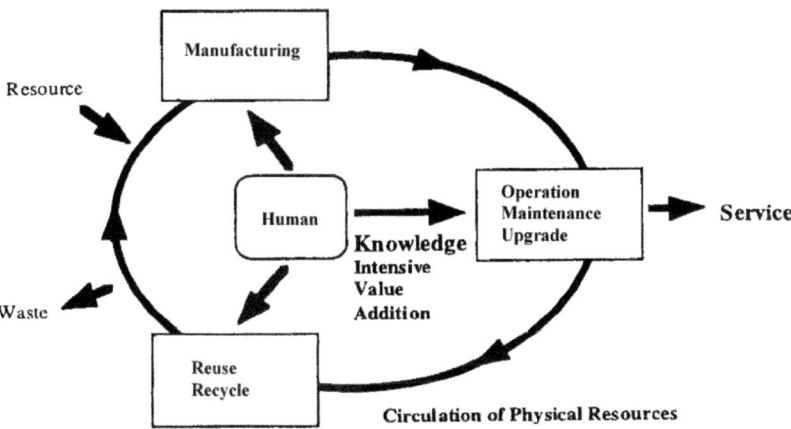

Fig. 6.1 New product and service development process

SERVICE LEVELS

Whatever is being produced and delivered, customers, clients and end users expect specific and expected levels of service, in support of the products and services that they are producing, delivering and making available.

Some organisations enter into service level agreements with their customers and clients, defining such critical issues as speed of response, minimum and maximum waiting times, replacement and returns policies and procedures. Others, especially IT and technology-driven companies, give assurances over performance and security. Mainstream retailers give 'no quibble' guarantees over all the products that they sell, whether or not they actually produced them.

Whatever the approach, people have to be assured that their expectations of value are going to be met. Directly related to this is the crucial and central question of quality.

QUALITY

Quality is one of those key words that is in turn: vital to every business, product and service; very hard to define; enhanced or devalued by every activity carried out; and informed by a large measure of collective and individual perception.

It is essential to be able to define quality in terms specific to every organisation, product and service. Pettinger (2011) defined quality as a function of the mixture of performance assurance, quantity, convenience, access, value and time in relation to any given product or service (including public services); and he also went on to state that customers' perceptions of quality and assurance were influenced by the wider reputation of the particular products or services in question. For example:

- Japanese cars and electrical goods always had (and have) the reputation for top and high quality. This is because people expect them to be of top and high quality, and so they look for the features that reinforce this perception;
- UK railway companies have a reputation for low quality and variable service, and so people look for the cues and signals that reinforce this perception;
- UK health and social care services are very good at the point of delivery, but not always easy to access in the first place, and so people look for these cues and signals also.

Dimensions of Quality

Ghylin et al. (2008) took this a stage further and defined four dimensions of quality as being: performance, features, reliability and conformance. They stated that so long as the product or service:

- performed as expected, promised or anticipated;
- had the features and functions that were promised or inferred in descriptions;
- was reliable in the specific and expected terms promised or inferred;
- conformed to specific standards of safety and security, and also met any expectations of kudos or status that went with ownership and/or usage;

people would be happy and satisfied.

In the pursuit of quality and assurance, and the value that is delivered as the result, technology and its contribution and performance are essential.

The roles that technology plays are critical; and these roles apply at every stage as follows:

- manufacturing is now delivered to more or less absolute standards. Components and finished articles are produced, assembled and delivered with more or less absolute provision at every stage;
- components that require maintenance or upgrades or replacement are now fully integrated into maintenance schedules;
- marketing and branding is now carried out in more or less real time through social media as well as traditional presentation and product and brand awareness techniques;
- people make up their minds very much more quickly as to the value that is delivered; and again they use social media to express their satisfaction or otherwise;
- products and services reservations, demands and purchases can now be made very much more quickly than previously, by virtue of web and internet access;
- there is a more or less universal access to product and service information in all sectors;
- people's perceptions and expectations are managed through social media, as well as through physical interactions with company staff and companies and organisations themselves;
- the availability of data and the ability to analyse it is turning marketing and new product and service development into a much more scientific part of organisation management than in previous times.

INSPECTION AND ASSURANCE

Quality assurance is underpinned by a combination of known, believed and perceived cues and triggers as above; and it is also assured at a statutory level by product and service inspections in all sectors.

How companies and organisations and their managers deliver on quality is very much a matter of choice and approach. It is essential to identify the key components of quality from the point of view of:

- organisation reputation;
- product and service reputation;

- service levels in support of delivering products and services;
- new product and service developments;
- developments and enhancements in service levels provided.

In the pursuit of providing valuable, excellent, durable and profitable products and services (and service) in all sectors, fully reliable transport and delivery systems are essential.

Conclusions

A fundamental reappraisal of what constitutes essential, desirable and valuable products and services is taking place as the result of the COVID19 pandemic. Because of the changes in the social as well as economic and technological environment, many products and services now no longer have the cachet or draw that they once enjoyed even a few months prior to the pandemic outbreak. Companies and organisations are now fully disposed towards conceptions of:

- rapid design, implementation and development;
- fail early and fail fast, where it is apparent or perceived that products and services are not going to deliver early and enduring results.

Where products and services are developed and made available for consumption, the overall design, execution, value and delivery processes have to be assured. As well as convenience, the outlets have to be demonstrably healthy and safe.

This is also true for public and social services. Hitherto unregarded issues on public transport and public facilities, including crowding, queueing, access and egress, have now become major focal points for individual and collective concern, again because of public health concerns. The shift in delivery of many services either in behavioural terms, or because they are now completely online, is causing collective and individual changes in attitudes and behaviour for those who use these services.

The ability of specific health and social care client groups to ask for services when and where these are needed is certain to add value to the provisions. This is from all points of view:

- the providers will be able to enhance their costs and charges;
- the clients will get services delivered at the time and location of requirement;
- there is the opportunity for business and services development, in terms of providing add ons that are known, believed and perceived to be of value to the client groups;
- as services are expanded and the add ons become familiar, this is likely to open up new markets and potential customer and client groups.

The ability to track goods and services is well established; and in time this will become absolute for everything. It will be possible to get universal real time information, and so scheduling and manufacturing of products and services will become more cost-effective in terms of volumes produced, locations delivered and made available. This scheduling will also be very much more accurate in terms of predictions and forecasting as data science and data analytics in all areas of business become more accurate and informed.

REFERENCES AND FURTHER READING

Edwards Deming, W. 2014. *Quality, Productivity and the Competitive Position*. MIT Centre for Advanced Engineering Study.

Garvin, D. 1987. *Competing on the Eight Dimensions of Quality*. HBR.

Ghylin, K.M., B.D. Green, C.G. Drury, J. Chen, J.L. Schultz, A. Uggirala, J.K. Abraham, and T.A. Lawson. 2008. Clarifying the Dimensions of Four Concepts of Quality. *Theoretical Issues in Ergonomics Science* 9 (1): 73–94.

Pettinger, R. 2011. *Contemporary Strategic Management*. Palgrave.

Pettinger, R. 2019. *Society Technology and Behaviour*. Studious/Ryze/UCL/UEA.

Stahel, W., and Reday, G. 1982. *Jobs for Tomorrow: The Potential for Substituting Manpower for Energy*. EU Publications.

https://www.ellenmacarthurfoundation.org/news/the-ellen-macarthur-foundation-signs-new-agreement-with-un-environment.

CHAPTER 7

Sustainability

Abstract This chapter introduces a clear perspective on sustainability from the points of view of business, society and technology. It draws attention to the need for much greater consideration and responsibility towards the whole cycle of resource usage and towards the attitudes required of companies and organisations in terms of sourcing, usage, waste management and disposal. The chapter identifies the leadership, management and organisational concerns that need to be addressed, as the world moves on from the COVID19 pandemic, and rebuilds economies, commerce and industry maximising and optimising the use of all resources.

Keywords Sustainability · Sustainability concerns · Triple bottom line · Waste · Sustainable work · Sustainable working patterns · Sectoral sustainability · Infrastructure development · Climate change · Social worth and value

INTRODUCTION

Sustainability is concerned with developing business, organisations and infrastructure for the good of all, without damaging the opportunities that future generations will need and want when their time comes.

At the core of this is the changing nature of the availability of resources, combined with the need to develop products and services that are going to have value for present and future generations, as well as contributing to the development of society. There are also issues around social, economic and industrial regeneration: the development of new industries and social fabric for areas and regions whose present activities are becoming obsolete.

Everything about this present position requires investment in activities and ventures—without any assurance of returns. It is therefore necessary to take a wider view of the commitment of resources at any given time and for any stated purpose:

- what else is this initiative or venture going to produce or deliver;
- what else might it deliver;
- what other industrial, social and economic developments in this a part of.

Specific decisions have to be taken also in terms of whether to create an infrastructure first, and then provide for social and economic development once it is there; or whether to create societies and centres of commercial activities first, and then build the infrastructure once the overall viability of the area is more or less assured (see Box 7.1).

Box 7.1 Sustainability: Some Definitions

People's perceptions of sustainability vary very greatly; and so here are some informative and concise statements that between them would give a detailed overview and starting point for understanding.

The ecological definition of sustainability originated with the Brundtland Report in 1987, which describes sustainable development as one that 'satisfies the needs of the present without adversely affecting the conditions for future generations' (Brundtland 1987).

Sustainability means 'meeting present and evolving human needs without compromising the ability of future generations to meet their own needs. In addition to natural resources, we also need social and economic resources. Sustainability is not just environmentalism. Embedded in most definitions of sustainability we also find concerns for social equity and economic development' (Sachs 2020).

> Environmental, social and economic sustainability: Sustainability is 'concerned with assuming that nature and the environment are not an inexhaustible resource and so, it is necessary to protect them and use them rationally. Sustainability promotes social development, seeking cohesion between communities and cultures to achieve satisfactory levels in quality of life, health and education. Thirdly, sustainability focuses on equal economic growth that generates wealth for all without harming the environment. Nowadays, many of the challenges that humans face such as climate change or water scarcity can only be tackled from a global perspective and by promoting sustainable development' (https://www.activesustainability.com/sustainable-development/what-is-sustainability/).

This then becomes the context in which organisation strategy, policies, priorities, operations and activities have to be implemented. Whatever the organisation's purpose and activities, there are major and more or less universal drives towards resource optimisation and assurance of availability.

Context

Sustainability is held to address four key concerns:

- resource usage and conservation;
- economic responsibility and viability;
- social responsibility and viability;
- environmental responsibility and viability.

For this context to be addressed and managed effectively, and so that the key concerns are tackled in full, further issues have to be established. These are:

- a triple bottom line, requiring that economic, social and environmental annual and quarterly reports are institutionalised and reported on;
- collective and individual behaviour has to be managed and modified and developed;
- viability is to attend to the long-term strength and security of the economic and social order, as well as to immediate concerns;
- viability is to attend to the good of all, as well as to individuals.

Strategy

The best, most profitable and most effective organisations are those which are clear about what they are doing, how, when, where and why they are doing it, and what they intend the results to be. This can only be achieved however, if a clear core or foundation position for activities and for competing is established; and this is because everything else emerges and is developed from the core or foundation position.

For the sake of clarity, organisations and their managers need to establish and agree the strategic foundation; and this is because if those who are responsible for the direction of organisations are not themselves clear, they cannot expect anyone else to be either. As in Chapter 3, the clarity of position emerges essentially from one of the following positions:

- cost leadership or advantage, where everything is driven by seeking to be the lowest cost or a low-cost operator in the sector;
- brand leadership or advantage, whereby products and services are differentiated through branding, identity and perceptions of quality and value;
- niche or specialisation, whereby a niche is identified, and the organisation then serves this to the best of its capabilities;
- something else, which must be capable of clear and accurate description.

This clarity gives the basis on which sustainability is to be based and developed. Above all this means reference to the long term, and the development of an organisation infrastructure and strength that will enable it to survive into the future, and will address whatever the chosen position is, with a wider and deeper range of responsibilities attached (see Box 7.2).

Box 7.2 Waste Disposal

Everyone agrees in principle that waste disposal and management is an issue of universal concern. The core problem arises from the following:

- who is to dispose of waste effectively;
- where and how waste is to be disposed of;

> – how to balance the legitimate and inevitable generation of waste (a universal by-product of all economic and social activity) against the legitimate demands, needs and wants of society.
>
> There is therefore a core leadership and management imperative in finding and defining the balance between engaging in essential, desirable and responsible human and economic activity.
>
> There are conflicting pressures. For example, on single use plastic and polystyrene products, there are:
>
> – legal issues that have to be addressed: many surgical and medical products and foodstuffs rely on single use plastic packaging to maintain their sterility and ability to use; and if the plastic packaging is either broken or damaged, then the product may not be used and has to be discarded;
> – social expectations, in that people are confident that anything that is packaged in single use plastics is germ and contamination free, and is therefore fit for use;
> – industrial growth and assurance: single use plastics are at the core of all bottled water and soft drinks production;
> – branding issues, in which food retailers rely on the presentation of fresh and preserved food products in single use plastic packaging and containers as they compete with other brands (who all do this also);
> – labelling and presentation and other branding activities, which again people expect to be in plastic.
>
> So plastic is a major economic resource, a driver of collective and therefore social assurance—and also a major and enduring polluter. Therefore social, economic and commercial drivers have to be reconciled with the need to preserve and limit resources consumption, and deliver products and services in a responsible as well as commercially viable way.

All organisations and their leaders and managers therefore need a common understanding and agreement on their organisational approach to sustainability. This requires:

– internal colloquy as the basis for agreeing the organisation position;

- external colloquy as the basis for delivering products and services in ways that are both acceptable in social terms, and also in relation to the position of people as customers, consumers and end users;
- attention to the key drivers and influences on present and future economic and social development.

Internal Colloquy

It is essential to realise that even when activities have been fully evaluated, and steps taken to gain collective agreement, this is only the first step in the engagement of expertise in strategic and operational sustainability management. Before a detailed evaluation and implementation plan can be considered, the capacity, capability and willingness of staff and their expertise have to be assessed. Existing processes and systems have to be capable of delivering what the agreed position on sustainability requires; or else new systems and processes (and patterns of behaviour and activities) have to be designed and integrated with what exists already.

Collective and individual staff perceptions have to be managed. This is less of a problem where there is a collective, cohesive and positive culture. However, major questions have to be addressed as to whether the position on sustainability is known, believed and perceived to be good and worthwhile; whether it is a necessary evil (in terms of having to work in particular ways to meet with specific legal, social or ethical concerns); whether it is indeed fundamentally good from all points of view; and whether ultimately it represents a step on the road to progress. Key and critical issues of where the resources are coming from, and how these are to be used and consumed, have to be addressed.

Especially, where there are operational consequences arising from changes to resource usage, must be made clear; and if the staff do not understand or support this, then they may resist the wider conceptions and overall approach to sustainability. This is compounded when such approaches require substantial changes to work locations, work patterns, job content and teams and groups; and so if and when such issues do arise, they have to be managed effectively (see Box 7.3).

Box 7.3 Working Remotely
Many organisations offer remote working (including working from home). This is very attractive to many, and has been embraced across a wide range of sectors. Many companies and organisations, and their staff, point out the real and perceived benefits of this:

- reduced numbers of journeys and travelling times;
- reduced non-productive time from the points of view of both not being able to work, and also not being able to do domestic things;
- reductions in fatigue and disruptions caused by the vagaries of transport networks;
- reductions in organisation premises required; and consequent reductions in energy, maintenance and replacement/refurbishment costs and consumption;
- reduced expenses on travelling and associated activities (e.g. car parking expenses; crèche costs for young children).

There is also a substantial collective and social reduction on transport networks and commuter routes; and this then becomes a contribution to overall social sustainability and reductions in resources consumption and expense.

There are caveats however:

- not everyone is willing to work in these ways; and so if it is required, it must be made clear to new starters that this is the basis on which operations are carried out;
- it is essential to consult in full when established staff are required to change their work patterns and habits;
- not everyone has suitable domiciles to work in these ways. People may and do have homes where there is no space to set aside as a work station, or where their patterns of life include extended family (e.g. young children; aged parents).

So staff required to work in these ways need to be fully supported and their wider circumstances understood, if they are to be involved in fully sustainable activities.

Remote working approaches also include working from flexible locations (e.g. hotels; business centres). Again it is essential to support people if they are required to work from such locations. It is usual to provide the

> technology and equipment required; and this includes assurances on the basics of streaming capacity and technology access and security.
>
> Additionally, it is essential to recognise that people are displaced from their social lives at work, and the human interactions that normally occur. Organisations are social as well as economically productive entities; and so anything that changes or removes this aspect of social being and belonging has to be recognised as an issue that has to be addressed and managed. It is essential that the benefits of flexible working are sustained; and so the drawbacks have to be noted, addressed and managed also.

External Colloquy

A detailed understanding is required of what external stakeholders are to make of what is proposed. Detailed knowledge and understanding is required of the likely and possible ranges of customer, client and end user responses. This is vital in terms of the new or proposed approaches. It is also vital in terms of the response to the existing range of products and services and how these are delivered at present: a critical issue to address is how any changes to processes implemented in the drive for sustainability is going to impact present operational relationships, and how these changes are going to be received by customers, clients, consumers and end users.

Shareholders have also to be satisfied that their returns will continue, ideally because of the new or proposed ways of doing things, and at least in spite of them. Shareholders need to know and understand the worst possible consequences, especially in the short term and transition periods. Shareholders normally need to be satisfied that they will at least get their money back over the long term. To that end they are entitled to see detailed forecasts and projections and are entitled to have questions answered, and any doubts and fears addressed. In particular, shareholders are entitled to be absolutely certain that their funds are not to be used in glamorous, exciting and untargeted ventures and adventures, without additionally being satisfied that there are commercially viable prospects and returns available also.

Key Sectors

The key sectors for the future are defined in terms of:

- population shifts and changing demographics, and the demands made by both migration and factors such as ageing, baby booms, changes in industrial and commercial bases;
- the physical, virtual and social development of business relationships all over the world and across borders;
- changing climate and environment, and how this is to be managed;
- use of resources (especially use of single use resources);
- social and economic cataclysms; including war zones and refugee crises; and including pandemics such as the COVID19 pandemic of 2020 and beyond.

With this in mind, key industrial and services sectors are defined as follows:

- Health care and the capability and willingness to make this available to all at the point of need. This includes access to treatment and pharmaceuticals whenever and wherever required; and this needs to be supported by ever improving testing, diagnostics and healthcare information management.
- Waste management and recycling, and investment in urban and rural regeneration; and this requires a fundamental collective social and economic shift of perspective on the part of companies, organisations, political establishments and society.
- Social care infrastructure, and recognition that this is a fundamental industry. It applies across the globe, and includes United Nations institutions, provisions for the displaced and excluded, as well as for local specific demographic groups (the disabled, elderly, homeless). This in turn requires a fundamental reappraisal and restructuring of social policies and collective social care approaches so that the organisations that deliver these activities are fully resourced, equipped and invested in.
- Energy generation and management, and recognition that a big part of this is to shift from central to local and individual generation. This is alongside a fundamental reappraisal of how energy is to be valued and charged for and costed.

- Infrastructure universality and quality. This requires regeneration in terms of universal access and assurance. It also means that ultimately IT and technology are to become utilities rather than commodities.
- Transport and distribution and infrastructure development. This is to maximise and optimise the opportunities for both social and also economic development. It is also to evaluate where new opportunities for social and economic—and technological—expansion and development are required (see Box 7.4).

Box 7.4 Infrastructure Development

As above, there are questions around whether the infrastructure drives economic and social development, or vice versa. There are examples from both sides, as follows:

- low-cost air travel has led to the development of economic activities as destinations have become popular;
- technology hubs have sprung up in overtly non-mainstream locations (e.g. Poland, Romania, Slovenia) because of clusters of technology expertise in those areas;
- some technology and engineering expertise is not being maximised or optimised (e.g. Tunisia) because of the lack of transport infrastructure;
- high speed rail links have seen social infrastructure and urban regeneration develop along their route networks (e.g. South East England; North Eastern France);
- long distance rail links are opening up social, economic and development opportunities along their route networks (e.g. the China/Trans Asia/Trans Europe freight routes);
- shipping ports are developing and regenerating old docklands environments as the size and value of containerised sea transport continues to grow.

In all of these examples, and whether the transport or society comes first, it is essential to provide 'a society'—housing and social provisions so that everyone has the best possible opportunity for a quality of life, as well as to be a part of economic activity.

Conclusions

The purpose here has been to look at the critical issues concerning sustainability and the need to manage the environment and within the environment; and to identify the issues that have to be addressed when developing the environment.

At the core of all of this is both social knowledge and understanding as well as economic and managerial and leadership expertise. In terms of sustainability, this emphasises the following:

- the relationship between economic and social demands and activities; and the need to integrate these demands and activities;
- the need for infrastructure development; and this means addressing the reuse of sites and machinery as well as the development of new sites and machinery.
- the need to address specific issues, especially waste management and energy production and generation.

It is also essential to look at and evaluate (and re-evaluate) regularly the foundations of economic and social activities and ensure that what is developed and instigated is of enduring as well as immediate economic value and worth. This in turn requires that everything is additionally evaluated from the point of view of its contribution to social worth and enduring impact on business as an integral part of the fabric of society.

References and Further Reading

Braun, E. 1998. *Technology in Context: Technology Assessment for Managers.* Earthscan.
Braun, E. 2014. *Futile Progress: Technology's Empty Promise* Earthscan.
Brundtland, G.H. 1987. *Our Common Future: World Commission on Environment and Development.* OUP.
Holmberg, J. 1992. *Making Development Sustainable.* Island Press.
Pettinger, R. 2002. *Managing the Flexible Workforce.* Cassell.
Pettinger, R. 2019. *Society Technology and Behaviour.* TIMTED Romania.
Sachs, J. 2015. *The Age of Sustainable Development.* Columbia.
Sachs, J. 2020. *The Ages of Globalization: Technology, Geography and Institutions.* Columbia.

CHAPTER 8

Ethics and Standards

Abstract This chapter introduces an overarching approach to the whole field of ethics and governance in organisations. It concentrates on specific and universal responsibilities in terms of: right and wrong; responsibilities and obligations; integrity; transparency; and governance. This area of organisational practice is of vital importance if companies and organisations in every sector are going to be able to produce and deliver goods and services in terms of the assurances, confidence and exactness that people have hitherto expected from being able to turn up to a physical outlet and get what they need and want.

Keywords Ethics and standards · Corporate Social Responsibility (CSR) · Responsibilities and obligations · Relationships · Corporate governance · Integrity · Conduct and behaviour · Shareholders' interests · Security · Right and wrong · Trust

Introduction

Ethics in business and management is concerned with those parts of organisational, operational, occupational and professional conduct that relate to absolute standards and principles in terms of conduct, behaviour and performance. Establishing standards requires reference to questions of: what is right and wrong in absolute terms; the desired ends and outcomes of any situation; and the ways and means by which the ends and outcomes are achieved. At the core of all business and managerial ethics are issues concerning: how the work is carried out; morality; integrity; judgement; and equality and fairness of treatment for all. Individual and collective conduct, behaviour and performance are regulated by law; and in turn regulated at places of work by legal compliance and management procedures which all organisations are required to have.

Business and managerial ethics and standards are established by all organisations in terms of:

- the nature of working, professional and personal relationships within the organisation;
- defining the quality of working life that they wish to have; and relating this to work practices, job content, and supervisory styles and approaches;
- compliance with commercial, social and employment law;
- financial reporting and financial probity and integrity;
- working effectively within the constraints of the social, cultural and religious customs in particular locations;
- corporate governance and corporate social responsibility (CSR);
- establishing a fundamental humanity at work, so that the professional and occupation output that is delivered, is achieved on a human as well as commercial basis;
- establishing strong, honest and substantial relations with all stakeholders.

Ethics Developed

Developing this position further, Sternberg (1990) states that: 'Business ethics applies ethical reasoning to business situations and activities'; and that it is therefore based on a combination of:

- organisational survival, in order to be able to deliver on its obligations to staff, stakeholders and the communities in which work is carried out;
- integrative justice: fundamentally treating everybody equally in human as well as employment and consumer terms;

- fairness and transparency in all dealings with people as employees, customers and suppliers;
- rewarding employees according to their contribution;
- ordinary common decency: a value judgement, capable of public justification, that is placed on all activities.

Adams et al. (1990) identify a series of factors and elements as issues against which the performance of organisations could be measured in ethical terms. These factors are:

- the nature of business, including operating in overtly contentious industries such as tobacco, alcohol, chemicals, armaments;
- the quality, integrity, availability and use of information;
- the nature of employment relationships and the extent to which staff are included as genuine stakeholders;
- relationships with emerging economies and markets;
- connections with governments and the integrity of dealings with governments and regimes.

There is therefore a great range of complexities and contradictions and contra indications that have to be taken into account when determining to establish standards of conduct, behaviour and performance. There are additional issues to be considered as follows:

- compliance with every aspect of business, commercial, employment, national and international law;
- attitudes to environmental issues, especially waste disposal and recycling; replenishing and replanting; the ways and means by which scarce resources are consumed;
- the nature of business relationships with suppliers and markets.

Additionally, every organisation generates information on a continuous basis. Because of technology, information has become a commodity, bought and sold between companies and organisations. This generates specific additional value and revenue streams as well as helping to ensure immediate and enduring financial viability. The sale and purchase of information is itself regulated by statutes and regulations at national and international levels.

Clearly, ethics in business and management is complex; and so it is important to establish where the complexities and conflicts lie in key situations, as follows:

- conduct, behaviour and performance that will be tolerated; and conduct, behaviour and performance that will not be tolerated; and this applies to every aspect of organisation conduct and behaviour; and defined approaches to staff relations and staff management;
- defined approach to customers and suppliers, so that everyone understands the business orientation of the organisation and its leaders and managers;
- defined approaches to backers, so that those who do have a financial interest and stake in the organisation understand the nature of the relationship that they will have;
- establishing a position and reputation in the business community;
- establishing a position and reputation in the locations where work is carried out.

It is additionally the case that people prefer to work for organisations that are as transparent and honest as possible; and people prefer to do business with organisations that conduct themselves to the highest possible standards.

Responsibilities and Obligations to Staff

Responsibilities and obligations to staff consist of providing work, remaining in existence, equality and fairness of treatment, compliance with the law, and providing a secure, healthy and safe working environment.

In order to do this, it is essential to acknowledge the range of pressures and priorities that exist in the lives of everyone. Especially in the post-pandemic world, where work patterns and habits and norms are fundamentally changing, it is essential to be able to discharge responsibilities in terms of:

- preserving confidentiality and integrity in all dealings with staff;
- ensuring a fundamental equality and equity of treatment of all staff, wherever and however they are working;

- ensuring that everyone gets the pay, benefits and rewards which are due to them, even if they do not turn up to work on the employer's premises;
- taking immediate steps to resolve staffing issues as soon as these become apparent; and addressing questions of performance standards, and other disputes, conflicts and grievances;
- ensuring that people work the hours required; and ensuring that remote working patterns do not lead to undue pressures of over work or under work;
- managing staff security, health, wellbeing and development, whatever their pattern and location of work.

In the post-pandemic world, and as technology advances, organisations and staff are increasingly demanding developments in work patterns. This in turn means attention to: where and how work is delivered; and working towards flexibility in terms of working hours. Additionally, organisations are having to change staffing priorities and management practices in terms of:

- acknowledging and discharging responsibilities and obligations to staff in terms of equipment and work spaces (whether at home, at business centres, or on flexible work spaces on employers' premises);
- recognising and addressing key issues of alienation, remoteness, isolation, lack of physical interaction and other changes in contact with colleagues, managers, subordinates and others;
- data protection and security and assurance of any technology and IT and data services required;
- access to legitimate work and other resources, including technology, IT and streaming, wherever and whenever work is carried out.

In previous times, all of these matters would be assured by going to a colleague or manager and asking. Under new organisational forms and structures and flexible working patterns, or work delivered away from organisation locations, these matters have to be addressed in ways that are suitable and effective.

Relationships with Suppliers

There used to be a received managerial wisdom, that it was good and effective practice to create 'a multiplicity of suppliers', because this would 'keep suppliers on their toes', and 'keep suppliers loyal'.

In practice, companies that adopt this approach actually show no loyalty to suppliers. They simply shop around, taking either the short-term view that they will accept deliveries from the lowest priced suppliers at the particular moment; or taking the expedient view that particular suppliers may be changed at will.

However, again because of changes post COVID19, a much clearer view is required of managing the supply side; and in many cases this means entering into assured and enduring relationships, even if this may put up the immediate costs of supplies. Many organisations have had to develop relationships with local and assured suppliers working on assured supply lines, rather than relying on cheaper supplies from much further away; and this is because of the disruptions and uncertainties caused by the COVID19 pandemic.

Relationships with Communities

The nature of community relations with organisations has changed in many aspects in response to the social changes around the COVID19 pandemic. As well as public health and social services, supermarkets and food shopping, transport and distribution are now recognised as core social as well as economic provisions.

Community confidence in their local businesses is founded in general feelings of social wellbeing that accrue as the result of having particular organisations located in specific communities. This is superficially wholly positive. However, it can and does bring particular ethical dilemmas: for example, nuclear power stations provide large volumes of high value and well paid work to their communities, and this has to be reconciled with continuing concerns and perceptions about radiation problems.

There are additional concerns in community relations as follows:

- Where a large organisation moves into a particular location and is able to poach staff from others already working there, because of its financial capability to provide substantially superior terms and conditions of employment;

- Where large firms are able to insist on specific development activities, to the known, believed or perceived detriment of the rest of the economic community. Of specific concern here is the development of out-of-town industrial and retail centres that are believed to damage or destroy the economic viability of centre-of-town activities;
- The ability of large organisations to avoid their core responsibilities, by ensuring that they have powerful financial and political support. In these cases, they are able to build and operate what they want from their own point of view and narrow self-interest, rather than what is in the wider interests of the particular community.

CORPORATE GOVERNANCE

Corporate governance is the term used to describe the constitution, processes, actions and priorities by which organisations are led, directed, regulated and developed. Corporate governance refers to the policies and practices that are present and in use. Corporate governance specifically identifies key responsibilities and expertise required of those in top, senior and key positions; and each of these sets an example for everyone else in the organisation to follow.

At the heart of corporate governance are fundamental questions of collective culture, conduct, behaviour and performance. Staff will take their lead from the ways in which top and senior managers conduct themselves. Especially, there is the fundamental issue of what is and is not tolerated in practice. If there is any question of wrong behaviour and actions being tolerated, these behaviours and actions quickly become 'not wrong'; and it is a further short step to these behaviours and actions becoming 'right'. This in turn leads to dilution of standards; and ambitious people will follow the pattern of behaviour that is known and understood to deliver rewards and progress.

Corporate governance is also concerned crucially with financial strength, probity and integrity. Top and senior managers must by law ensure financial transparency at all times. All companies and organisations must produce audited accounts that are a true and fair reflection of their financial conduct over the past period, and that underpin specific plans and initiatives for the future.

Standards of Conduct and Behaviour

Standards of conduct and behaviour are set around each of the following:

- managing shareholders' interests; and managing other stakeholders' interests;
- financial conformance and probity and integrity;
- working within the law in all activities;
- setting and maintaining absolute standards of probity and integrity in all activities;
- establishing clarity in rewarding top and senior managers.

Top and senior managers set the standards for the conduct and behaviour of the organisation as a whole; and functional managers, section heads and supervisors do the same for their own people. The core issues are as follows:

- if top management set lax standards, there is ultimately little point in those lower down the organisation trying to set high standards;
- if top management set high standards, then the extent to which these are absolute in practice is a direct reflection of what happens when those lower down the organisation allow standards to slip.

Managing Shareholders' Interests

The priority in managing shareholders' interests is communication. Shareholders and their representatives need to know and understand the nature of returns on offer; the conditions under which returns are possible; and the changes in conditions likely to affect these returns. This is so that shareholders, and their representatives, know and understand where top management is taking the organisation, and why, in terms of financial returns. It also provides shareholders, and their representatives, with a key point of reference in their dealings with top management; and ultimately, if they do not like what top management is doing, shareholders' representatives will replace them.

Technology

Technology standards and the policies that enforce them are founded in a wealth of data protection and security assurance legislation. Technology policies have to deal with critical business and human concerns around:

- Security;
- Connectivity assurance;
- Integrity of those who operate systems and data bases;
- Methods for the gathering, storage and retrieval of data;
- Data use and misuse/abuse;
- Data as a commodity to be bought and sold;
- Rights and duties to privacy of individuals and groups;
- Rights to protection of individual and everything to do with their lives and circumstances.

There are major challenges in this part of management and organisation practice. It is in practice virtually impossible for people to guarantee their privacy in overall terms, if they have any online, social or digital media presence or activity, or if they own any mobile devices; and this is compounded if people are required to work extensively with technology and streaming systems. With shifts to ever greater online and remote working, there is a major organisational issue and a key priority for management in ensuring that staff do get afforded the maximum possible security and privacy, and that no personal privacy breaches occur as the result of being online for work purposes.

Corporate Social Responsibility (CSR)

Corporate social responsibility (CSR) is a statement of initiative and commitment made by companies and organisations towards contributing to the wider social and cultural life around them. CSR activities include making charitable commitments, sponsoring events, and giving resources to social projects and initiatives as a part of developing wider community relations and seeking to give something to the locations in which they work.

CSR is partly brand building, in that all actions taken are recognised and used to develop awareness of the organisations. CSR is also partly a response to acknowledging all organisations' wider and enduring commitments to society; and in the post-COVID19 world, many organisations are going to come under pressure to make further social contributions, as other sources of money and resources dry up.

Right and Wrong

Differentiating right and wrong is not as straightforward as it might overtly appear. It is often very difficult to define absolutes of right and wrong; and even when this is possible, it does not always set absolute standards. There is a mixture that all managers and leaders need to be aware of as follows:

- doing the right things for the right reasons;
- doing the right things for the wrong reasons;
- doing the wrong things for the right reasons;
- doing the wrong things for the wrong reasons.

Doing the right things for the right reasons is straightforward. Otherwise, dilemmas and contradictions and contra indications arise as follows.

In terms of doing the right things for the wrong reasons, individuals may take correct and effective business decisions in the knowledge that the outcome will also impact favourably on their careers. Companies and organisations carry out layoffs or close down specific activities in order to preserve their share price or stay within budget, or because it is easier than doing a full appraisal of the organisation's overall position.

Doing the wrong things for the right reasons is more complex. If managers dismiss employees to make an example of them, and if the employees did not deserve dismissal, then a wrong act is committed even if it brings the remaining staff into line. If the organisation secures its long-term future through gaining a contract by offering a bribe to a major customer, then a wrong act is committed. If under pressure managers encourage their staff to cut corners in order to speed up output, this is wrong also.

In cases such as this, companies, organisations and managers may secure a short-term advantage; and if they are lucky they may not have to face any consequences. It is a very risky approach however; and when such acts are discovered there are always adverse consequences.

Conclusions

Business and managerial ethics is a major and core field of study. As above, ethics pervades every aspect of organisational life and business practice and conduct. This is certain to become of ever greater significance as so much work is transferred from organisation premises to remote working; and so much commerce is transferred away from physical premises to online provision.

This is because everyone—staff, customers and suppliers—have to be able to trust those with whom they do business. Face to face transactions always enabled the position of trust to be built up at and during the point of meeting. This trust position has now to be built up online in many more cases than previously. It is therefore essential that organisations and their leaders and managers commit to the highest possible standards of integrity, conduct, behaviour and performance.

References and Further Reading

Adams, T., J. Hamil, and S. Carruthers. 1990. *Changing Corporate Values*. Earthscan.
Frysel, B. (ed.). 2017. *The True Meaning of CSR*. Palgrave.
Griseri, P., and N. Seppala. 2010. *Business Ethics and Corporate Social Responsibility*. Cengage.
Idowu, S.O., et al. (eds.). 2018. *Corporate Social Responsibility and Governance: Theory and Practice*. Springer.
Lim, A., and Y. Tsutsui (eds.). 2015. *Corporate Social Responsibility in a Globalizing World*. Cambridge.
Sternberg, E. 1990. *Just Business*. Warner.

CHAPTER 9

Technological Development

Abstract The purpose of this chapter is to look at key technological developments and how they enhance and drive business development (and how in some cases they limit and diminish business development). It is necessary to know and understand the technologies that leaders, entrepreneurs and managers may choose to work with; and those also that they find themselves having to work with. This has to be seen from the perspective that the post COVID19 world is certain to be very much more driven by technology in every aspect. People are now very much more used to: working from home; shopping from home; and this is becoming a new norm as well as substantial social and organisational change. Above all, people are now very used to working from home and conducting business and social meetings and events via technological link, rather than travelling to and attending places of work in person.

Keywords Technology inclusion and exclusion · Technology development · Technology infrastructure · Technology and social value · Disruption · Obsolescence · Technology impacts on work · Work life balance · Supervision · Social aspects of work patterns and habits · Obsolescence

Introduction

The purpose of this chapter is to look at key technological developments and how they enhance and drive business development (and how in some cases they limit and diminish business development). It is necessary to know and understand the technologies that leaders, entrepreneurs and managers may choose to work with; and those also that they find themselves having to work with.

It is essential that all managers, leaders and entrepreneurs make themselves as fully familiar with all technological developments as possible. This is because every development generates a change in the operating environment. Every change brings about opportunities, threats and consequences for the existing products, services, markets and ways of working.

Technological change is also certain to become much more of a driving force in all COVID19 pandemic and post-pandemic activities, in terms of its contribution to the wider business environment and to the ways in which all markets operate, as well as becoming major and critical features of organisation structure and infrastructure, as well as being sources of information and communication.

Technology Development

The driving forces in technology development are founded in the human, commercial and social demands for ever greater convenience, assurance and security in every aspect of life. Sourcing technology development in all of its forms depends on the capability, willingness and commitment of those involved.

There is also a great deal of cross development and co-development. For example:

- Defence tracking technology has been developed to provide major service advantages to such diverse operations as: commercial flight tracking; postal services; domestic delivery services; insurance claim management; and emergency situation responses;
- Motor racing technology is used to inform the development and reliability of motor car engines;
- Laser technology is used to develop the accuracy of the instruments used in medical and surgical procedures.

There are many others. One part of the ability to advance product, services, service and infrastructure development in any field is therefore to be as aware as possible of everything going on everywhere, and to be able to evaluate for applications, modifications and deliverables in any other area (see Box 9.1).

Box 9.1 Science Fiction
Many people are inspired towards technology development as the result of interests in science fiction.

Orthia (2019) notes the effects of science fiction on overall approaches to technology development, in a study carried out among Doctor Who fans. She stated that:

- people were influenced to think about scientific development as the result of having seen things on Doctor Who;
- people were also disposed to think about the general ethical and moral issues around technology and its influences; and what people thought addressed both good and bad issues;
- it also had a marginal effect on the numbers of people deciding to take up scientific careers; and those who did take up scientific careers as the result remained committed to science for the whole of their lives.

Orthia's work also noted that there are key general influences from science fiction that have to be seen in overall approaches to technological development. Many inventions resemble things that have been seen in science fiction films. For example:

- Speaking computers and interactive screens;
- Artificial limbs;
- Design and appearance of spaceships;
- Computer-driven medical and surgical instruments.

were all found in science fiction long before they became fact; and their development bears a great resemblance to what was originally presented by the science fiction film makers.

Technological Infrastructure in a Business and Social Context

There is more or less universal access to the existing and developing technological infrastructure, although clearly the quality of that infrastructure and the connectivity that it delivers, varies between countries, regions and localities. A key priority is therefore to ensure that there is sufficient bandwidth, streaming capacity and overall connectivity assurance for all; and this is an ever greater priority in a pandemic and post-pandemic environment. Many organisations and institutions are calling for IT and streaming capacities to be viewed as public utilities.

Alongside the drive for capacity, and for the present and for the foreseeable future, therefore, inventions and developments are to contribute to the present and envisaged needs, wants, demands and drives, as follows:

- disruption in all sectors;
- development of emerging markets and locations;
- specific inventions and developments in areas of key importance and value to humanity;
- contributions to social infrastructure;
- integration of new and existing technologies;
- changes and developments in job and work opportunities;
- the integration of personal, professional and occupational development into both work patterns and also work/life balances;
- the integration of learning and development into all aspects of work and organisation practice and operations.

This is likely to make the employment of staff a much greater and more engaging and engaged commitment than exists in many organisations at present. The speed of technological change and advancement means that those who do not commit to continuous learning, training and development, are certain not to be able to take full advantage of the opportunities that come along; and this applies to both organisations and also to individuals.

In the pandemic and post-pandemic world of 2020 and beyond, a clear operational priority is to shift as much work as possible to being technology driven and carried out in remote locations (including homes and business centres). This reinforces the need for ever increasing capacity and bandwidth. It also reinforces the demands for:

- job and work and occupation design and redesign;
- approaches to product and service developments;
- creation and management of project and work teams;
- the need for, and development of, human interaction technology, so that meetings can be easily, quickly and effectively constituted whenever required;
- personal and collective ordering and delivery services on an ever increasing scale so that people can do their jobs (as well as using the ordering services for their wider lives).

JOB, WORK AND ORGANISATION OBSOLESCENCE

It follows from the above that there are certainties in job, work and organisation obsolescence. There is nothing new in this: job, work and organisation obsolescence are universal by-products of technological, social and economic advancement and development; and this too can be traced back thousands of years. The result is two fold:

- existing jobs and occupations evolve and develop;
- those who are in jobs and occupations that are genuinely obsolete have to find other work and/or retrain.

What replaces the obsolescent jobs and work is crucial; and this also is from a social as well as economic point of view. From an operational and economic point of view, for example:

- mechanics who used to repair engines now replace parts;
- people who used to build engineering products now assemble components (and in many cases watch components being assembled by machines);
- sales people now work wherever the work takes them, including working out of cars, hotels, business centres, airports, rather than an office;
- customer services staff now work in call centres rather than face to face.

From a social point of view, there are issues relating to status and respect that have to be addressed. These issues include:

- the standing in which previous occupations were held, relative to the present job and work;
- the value placed on the new jobs and occupations;
- the wages and salaries commanded by new jobs and occupations, both in absolute terms and also in relation to the old;
- availability of skills and expertise in the new jobs, and the extent to which staff have to be trained by particular organisations, or that they can be bought in ready to work;
- the social standing of present and new jobs and occupations, and the extent to which people do and will aspire to have and deliver the expertise required;
- the extent to which new jobs and occupations give opportunities for self and collective development.

There are also critical changes to the ways in which people live and work, and the balance of time spent in and away from work. To date, the standard pattern was that people 'went to work' somewhere away from home. The journey to and from work produced comfortable and assured patterns of life and behaviour, social interactions and contacts, and gave human confidence and assurance as well as a standard and familiar pattern of behaviour, the return on which was economic gain.

This is now changing; and it is certain that it will never again revert to the previous ways. While many jobs and occupations are certain to require physical attendance for all or part of the time, the opportunities offered by technology and organisation practice give people the opportunity to work in much more flexible ways. These opportunities also deliver a much greater capability to mix in work with all of the other demands of life, without affecting overall work performance.

SPECIFIC ISSUES

There are specific issues that have to be understood. These issues relate centrally to the needs of managers and organisations to know and understand the value that technology delivers, how to value the value, and where that value lies within the organisation. These technologies are central to delivering new working environments and activities, and the new patterns of work and occupations which go with them.

All organisations are going to be faced with using and implementing any, and in some cases, all new technologies as they become available and prove or demonstrate their capacities and value. This in turn means that a key part of managerial and leadership expertise now becomes:

- environmental scanning with particular reference to technological invention and development, assessing everything that comes along for potential usage and value;
- financial awareness in relation to technology, assessing costs and benefits for production, services, service delivery and organisation utility and infrastructure;
- financial awareness in relation to valuing the technology and the benefits that are delivered;
- operational awareness in terms of capacity and universality of usage;
- making external users, especially suppliers and customers, aware of any changes to operating practices and web capabilities as required;
- risk management, in terms of assessing new and existing technologies for capacity, security, assurance of performance and staff management issues (including training and development);
- data management, in terms ensuring that what is held and used is factually accurate, comprehensive and only used for the purposes for which it was gathered;
- potential disruptions to operations when new technologies do have to be introduced, developed or upgraded;
- staff evaluation, in terms of their capability and (crucially) willingness to use new technologies as they become available;
- staff management in terms of specific training and development, job redesign, job and work obsolescence, and new jobs and occupations;
- staff management in terms of delivering appropriate and effective supervisory approaches and activities to and for those who work remotely.

None of this changes the fundamental leadership and managerial expertise required. It does however mean that the application of that expertise is repositioned and needs to be effective in a much changed working, operational, commercial and social environment. Especially, there are fundamental changes to how control is exercised; how managers gain access to their staff so that supervision is effective; and more generally how to manage inclusion and exclusion.

Supervision

The key aspects of supervision—reporting relationships, target setting, communication and performance management—remain as critical as ever. These activities now have to be delivered in a remote and flexible manner in response to the changing and changed ways of working. This means that channels of communication have to be assured at all times; and this is to be reinforced through complete transparency of working methods and performance management approaches that allow for the staff to work in their own ways, ask questions at any time, and get supportive and positive feedback at any time, both on work in progress and also once work is completed and delivered.

It is not possible to replicate the physical environment online. Some organisations in the early stages of the COVID19 crisis tried to ensure a form of presenteeism by simply insisting that all staff logged on to one of the platforms available (e.g. Skype, Zoom), and remained visible to managers and supervisors throughout their working days. This is not feasible. Neither is it the best use of technology; doing this for its own sake is simply cluttering up the platform and detracting from the capacity available to those who do need it.

It follows from this that, even in the most adversarial of working environments, supervisors are going to have to learn to trust their staff very much more, to work when required, and to deliver the results expected and demanded.

Inclusion and Exclusion

In every aspect of technology, there are questions and issues of inclusion and exclusion. This is not new; every major technological invention and development has had such issues in the past e.g.:

- the first airliners provided exclusive service and were very expensive to travel in;
- the first cars were very expensive and hard to purchase (because there were not enough of them);
- the first items of what are now mainstream and assured products (washing machines, televisions/colour televisions, mobile phones, laptop computers) were expensive, unreliable and hard to use.

This reinforces a key feature of new products and services development: that early adopters who buy into something for early usage advantage also act as de facto maintainers, developers, guinea pigs and reviewers, contributing to product and service knowledge, fault finding and overall improvement, as companies and organisations seek to get something that is fully viable on to the market.

In terms of using a technologically driven infrastructure, inclusion and exclusion takes a different form. In order to be able to use some of the key services provided online and as the result of SMART developments, it is necessary to have access to the IT and internet/web and other networks as a precondition. This is not available to some sections of society, and the reasons for this are:

- lack of connectivity in specific locations;
- choice, either of the company or organisation (which is very unusual), or of parts of the client bases for their own reasons (lack of trust of the technology; privacy);
- cost, either because it is prohibitively expensive to particular sections of the community, or because some sections choose not to pay the charges anyway;
- availability of hardware which can be expensive and of limited connectivity and performance;
- access to networks, which are normally commercially operated and which can therefore price sectors of society out of affordability;
- compatibility of operating systems, especially those that operate on local networks and servers;
- complexity of software and programmes, which may lose connectivity with others due to specific operating issues. Software complexity and interconnectivity may also cause security issues at the linkage points.

There are therefore issues for companies and organisations to address if they do want people to have access to the facilities that they are developing. Companies may take a variety of views on this, as follows:

- the infrastructure is for the IT and telecommunications and technology companies; the residual responsibilities for other companies

is only to ensure that their own technologies are compatible with and secure in relation to the infrastructure provided;
- the infrastructure is a core public service sector utility and responsibility, akin to that for the railways and roads, and so it is up to local and central government and their agencies to provide a sound and secure basis for all activities;
- if companies want and need their suppliers and customers to be able to access them through networks, then they have an enduring responsibility to ensure that the infrastructure as well as their own systems remain fit for purpose;
- they may push the infrastructure responsibility back on to the customers and suppliers, taking the position that if others need and want to do business with them, then it is their responsibility to ensure full connectivity.

Whichever position is adopted comes with commitments to ensure that everything works as it should, and ensuring also that everyone has the access that they require. This is of critical importance and value in the pandemic and post pandemic world; connectivity has to be secure, assured and capable of access by everyone at any time.

Conclusions

The value brought by technology has to be capable of understanding from an organisational point of view. In all of the areas stated above technology should add value by:

- providing assured connectivity;
- providing completeness of service;
- ensuring universal access and availability on demand and necessity;
- ensuring completeness of provision.

If any of these factors are not present, technology dilutes value. Questions of accessibility have to be addressed in terms of inclusion and exclusion; and as above this means that people have to be able to afford connectivity as well as having physical access. The idea has been floated in the UK and elsewhere of making broadband universally available and free at the point of usage, and this would satisfy one part of access and inclusion were it to happen.

It follows from this that it is also necessary to understand how people come to think of technology advances. Organisations and institutions need to develop the best possible products, services, service and infrastructure; and the socio-economic view again reinforces that the social demand has to be integrated as fully as possible if the potential of technology is to be maximised and optimised.

REFERENCES AND FURTHER READING

Carlson, A.L. 2018. *Women in STEM: Critical Essays*. Simon & Schuster.

Ede, A. 2019. *Technology and Society: A World History*. Cambridge University Press.

Labour Party of Great Britain. 2019 *Manifesto*. Cooperative Publications.

Norgate, S.H., and C.L. Cooper (eds.). 2020. *Flexible Working: Designing Our Healthier Future Lives*. Routledge.

Orthia, L. 2019. *Dr Who, Science Fiction and Science Fact*. BBC.

Rosen, L., N. Cheever, and L.M. Carrier. 2015. *The Wiley Handbook of Psychology, Technology and Society*. Wiley.

CHAPTER 10

Leadership

Abstract This chapter reviews the key areas of all the major leadership studies and definitions to date, and from this proposes a leadership approach that addresses all of the key organisational demands and responsibilities—and accountabilities—placed on those in top, senior and key positions. The chapter reinforces the need for leadership qualities and expertise in the present and evolving environment. The chapter draws a distinction between expert and non-expert leaders, and the effects that each has on their business and operations, and on the people to whom they are accountable.

Keywords Leadership · Situational leadership · Leadership expertise · Leadership roles · Leadership styles · Leadership authority · The leadership difference

INTRODUCTION

Leadership is required in all areas of every organisation. It is becoming increasingly essential to be able to legitimately assign responsibility, authority and accountability to those in charge of organisations, and those who head individual departments, divisions and functions.

It is increasingly difficult, and in some cases impossible, to sustain the expense incurred of having large and complex hierarchical and bureaucratic systems for the coordination and control of organisations. This has been the case for a long time, and the financial pressures of the COVID19 pandemic have brought the need to manage this expense to a critical position.

Employing people with leadership expertise in key and critical positions and functions therefore reduces expense; and it additionally leads to clearer lines of authority and accountability, resulting in increased output, delivered more quickly, and with fewer problems and barriers.

- to give vision and direction;
- to energise, motivate and drive everything and everyone in every set of circumstances;
- to set and enforce absolute standards of behaviour, attitude, presentation and performance;
- to deliver the performance required by the organisation's strategy, vision and direction;
- to instill confidence in everyone;
- to accept responsibility and accountability for both successes and failures;
- to address any crises and emergencies;
- to act as the focal point for the organisation in dealings with all stakeholders;
- to reflect the company and organisation identity, both internally, and also in external dealings.

In this context, the key role and function is having the combination of expertise, commitment and personality required to see things through to completion. It is additionally essential that leaders surround themselves with expertise that they themselves do not have so that any gaps in their own shortcomings are filled.

Leadership Expertise

The ability and expertise of all those in leadership positions is founded in their ability to establish, maintain and develop their own authority; to cope with change and uncertainty; and to deal effectively with the wide range of stakeholders who have an interest in what the organisation does. Leaders must be able to see the organisation's potential for development and advancement, and to take actions that deliver ever-improving performance. Leaders must also in all situations:

- harness technology productively;
- establish good internal processes, with especial reference to planning, budgeting, information systems and forecasting;
- be expert communicators;
- choose good staff and subordinates;
- encourage and reward initiative, excellent performance, targeted performance and advancement; and deal effectively with poor performance;
- deal with stresses and difficulties whenever these arise.

Above all, leaders must deliver the results expected, anticipated and demanded. Results are measured in terms of what was intended, and the actual outcomes; how and why these were achieved; how they were viewed at the time and subsequently by posterity; and whether this represented a good, bad or indifferent return on the resources and energy expended in their pursuit. Leaders are responsible and accountable for successes and failures.

Leaders are made, not born. The expertise of leadership has to be identified and developed by each individual who aspires to any position of authority and direction in every field.

Traits, Characteristics and Qualities

Attempts to identify the traits and characteristics present in successful leaders are largely inconclusive, in that none identify all the attributes necessary to lead, direct or manage in all situations. However, the following are more or less universal.

- Communication: the ability to communicate with all people with whom the leader comes into contact regularly, continuously and in ways and language in which those on the receiving end will both be able to understand and to respond to.

- Decision-making: the ability to take the right decisions in given situations, to take responsibility and be accountable, and to understand the consequences of particular courses of action.
- Commitment: to immediate matters in hand and also the wider aspects of the organisation as a whole. This includes willingness at all times to draw on personal, as well as professional, energies and to bring qualities of enthusiasm, drive and ambition on every occasion.
- Concern for staff: respecting, trusting and committing to the staff at all times; developing them, understanding them and their aspirations whatever their occupation. Staff must always be treated on a basis of equality and confidence.
- Quality: a commitment to the quality of products, services and service so that customers receive high value and satisfaction.
- Values: leaders bring a given set of values with which others will identify. These values are founded in personal and professional integrity, and the establishment of high absolute standards of conduct and performance required and demanded.
- Charisma: charisma is developed and manufactured through the combination of: expertise; personality; presentation; and identity; so that the result is positive and inspirational to all.

Leadership Styles

It is usual to identify leadership styles as being:

- positive autocratic, in which it is very clear who is in charge; however the leader works on a basis of harmony and development;
- negative or tyrannical autocratic, in which the leader is both oppressive and threatening to those who work for them;
- participative and consultative, in which the leader will always inform and discuss matters with the staff before arriving at a decision. The decision may or may not be influenced by the discussions with the staff;
- democratic leadership, in which the organisation proceeds in the direction determined by the majority. Superficially attractive, democratic leadership is only effective if in practice there is always an informed consensus and unanimity about the ways to proceed. Also, if there is only ever a narrow majority in favour of any course of

action, there will always be a high proportion of people disaffected whatever is decided.

It is essential to note that leadership styles have to change as organisations develop. For example, the inspirational, actively involved and full engaged leadership of a small pioneering enterprise necessarily has to change if that company becomes successful and staff numbers grow. It is not possible to be involved as fully with several hundreds of staff as it is with just one or two. It is therefore essential to recognise that leadership style has to evolve, both in relation to the organisation and also in relation to the overall operational environment.

Leadership styles are then seen in their organisational context, which is one or more of the following:

- Pioneer: pioneers and pioneering leaders establish and create new products, services, brands, ventures and markets. Pioneers have a clear vision of what is possible, and through their commitment, energy, enthusiasm and ambition, they use their expertise to create and energise whatever is proposed, and see it into existence, effectiveness and profitability. Pioneers may however become ineffective once a particular venture is established, secured and viable.
- Transformational: transformational leaders undertake major initiatives and ventures on behalf of organisations that require 'transforming' in some way. Often appointed purely to see the particular initiative through, transformational leaders must be able to assimilate and become authoritative, comfortable and familiar in a new organisational setting very quickly and effectively.
- Corporate: corporate leaders are the appointed to serve the interests of primary and dominant stakeholders; and this normally means the shareholders and their representatives. Problems arise when the returns to shareholders are not made for some reason. Problems additionally arise when someone who has been successful in one industry or company and is engaged on that basis in another industry, subsequently encounters problems in the new organisation.
- Strategic: strategic leaders are engaged because of their capability in seeing and envisioning the direction that a company or organisation ought to take over the medium to long term. The key need for strategic leaders is the ability to engage the quality and standing of

expertise required to translate the vision and strategy into action and achievement.
- Operational: operational leaders are those who provide clear leadership and direction to those who work for them, when working to a clear remit given to them by the organisation.
- Problem-solver and crisis leader: problem-solvers and crisis leaders are appointed to get an organisation out of a mess. Problems and crises may relate to stock market, product or service performance; or to scandals, negligence or incompetence. The key here is to address and resolve the particular problem, while at the same time maintaining morale and reputation. It is no use solving one problem but then either creating or else leaving others.

There then arises the question of who is best in each of the above situations. Some individuals are effective in all of these positions. Other organisations need to change their leadership as and when they grow, develop, retrench and change. Some leaders are only good at one aspect or part and so need to hand over to others when they have made their contribution.

Leadership Roles

The main leadership roles are as follows.

Figurehead and ringmaster: the leader acts as the human face of the department, division or organisation at all times. The key to being an effective figurehead is extensive preparation, consistent presence and visibility, and the development of high-quality communication skills.

Ambassador: leaders act as ambassador, advocate, enthusiast, cheerleader and problem-solver on the part of their department, division, organisation and staff. Everyone who plays this role requires expert briefing and preparation, as well as sound knowledge and understanding of the overall situation.

Servant: in which the manager is the ultimate supporter or servant of staff, product and service output and quality, and markets, customers and clients.

Maintenance role: requiring:

- daily maintenance: attending to problems and issues as they arise;
- preventative maintenance; continuous improvement of the work, working environment and procedures and practices; and attending to staff development also;
- breakdown maintenance: handling crises, blow-ups and storms in a quick and effective manner.

Role model: leaders, managers and supervisors set the style, standards, attitudes and behaviour for those who work for them. If leaders show qualities of commitment, enthusiasm, energy and honesty, these may be expected and be demanded from subordinates.

The role elements are a critical factor of leadership expertise. Every leader has to be able to take these roles from time to time. Capability in each role is essential to successful and effective leadership and direction at whatever level. To be an effective leader there is an overwhelming responsibility placed upon the individual to adopt these roles and the responsibilities inherent within them. It is also incumbent upon the person concerned to develop any of the qualities required in which they are not proficient.

Those who aspire to leadership positions must therefore be prepared to accept that there are certain qualities that go with the job—above all, enthusiasm, ambition, clarity of purpose, energy and direction—and must be prepared to develop these as the condition of employment in these positions. It is also important to recognise that this part of management development cannot be achieved except through the period of long-term prioritised intensive and demanding training, supported with periods of further education either at a university or conducted through the private sector. It is impossible to develop leaders purely on the basis of single or isolated short periods of training, unsupported by activities at the workplace. The best practitioners of particular trades, professions or occupations do not necessarily make the best leaders and managers of groups of these staff; assessment for leadership and management potential must be carried out on the basis of the ability to observe the leadership qualities required, rather than existing professional, occupational and technical expertise.

It is clear that leadership development is going to become very much more important in the future. Organisations are certain to value much more highly the all-round capabilities and willingness to accept responsibility on those whom they place in top positions.

Contingency Approaches

Contingency and 'best fit' theories of leadership take account of the interaction and interrelation between the organisation and its environment. This includes the recognition, and accommodating of, those elements that cannot be controlled. It also includes recognising that those elements that can be controlled and influences must be addressed in ways that vary in different situations—that the correct approach in one case is not a prescription to be applied to others. There is a constant interaction between the leader's job and the work to be done; and between this and the general operations of the organisation in question. There is also the requirement to vary the leadership style according to the changing nature of the situation.

Fiedler (1967) used the contingency approach to identify situations where directive and prescriptive styles of leadership and management worked effectively. Directive and prescriptive styles could be engaged where the overall situation was very favourable to the leader; where the leader was liked, respected and trusted by the group. Tasks needed to be clearly understood, easy to follow and well defined. The leader needed to have a high degree of influence over group members in terms of reward and punishment, and also unconditional support from the organisation.

Leaders have to be action-oriented; and this applies to those in leadership positions in all organisations, in all sectors. Taking action means that some things will go well; and on other occasions, mistakes will be made. No leader is successful every time. It is essential however, to learn, and learn quickly, from mistakes. It is essential to study and evaluate the performance of other leaders in other sectors; and from this, to analyse and evaluate the reasons why they were successful in some sets of circumstances but not others (see Box 10.1).

Box 10.1 Leaders and Non-leaders
Peters and Austin (1988) identified a long and comprehensive list of factors present in a 'leader'; and they contrasted this with the mirror attributes of the 'non-leader'.

Leader	Non-Leader
• Carries water for people	• Presides over the mess
• Open door problem-solver, advice giver, cheerleader	• Invisible, gives orders to staff, expects them to be carried out
• Comfortable with people in their workplaces	• Uncomfortable with people
• No reserved parking place, dining room or lift	• Reserved parking place and dining table
• Manages by Walking About	• Invisible
• Arrives early, stays late	• In late, usually leaves on time
• Common touch	• Strained with 'inferior' groups of staff
• Good listener	• Good talker
• Available	• Hard to reach
• Fair	• Unfair
• Decisive	• Uses committees
• Humble	• Arrogant
• Tough, confronts nasty problems	• Elusive, the 'artful dodger'
• Persistent	• Vacillates
• Simplifies	• Complicates
• Tolerant	• Intolerant
• Knows people's names	• Doesn't know people's names
• Has strong convictions	• Sways with the wind
• Trusts people	• Trusts only words and numbers on paper
• Delegates whole important jobs	• Keeps all final decisions
• Spends as little time as possible with outside directors	• Spends a lot of time massaging outside directors
• Wants anonymity for himself, publicity for the company	• Wants publicity for himself
• Often takes the blame	• Looks for scapegoats
• Gives credit to others	• Takes credit
• Gives honest, frequent feedback	• Amasses information
• Knows when and how to discipline people	• Ducks unpleasant tasks

(continued)

(continued)

Leader	Non-Leader
• Has respect for all people	• Has contempt for all people
• Knows the business and the kind of people who make it tick	• Knows the business only in terms of what it can do for him/her
• Honest under pressure	• Equivocation
• Looks for controls to abolish	• Looks for new controls and procedures
• Prefers discussion rather than written reports	• Prefers long reports
• Straightforward	• Tricky, manipulative
• Openness	• Secrecy
• As little paperwork as possible	• As much paperwork as possible
• Promotes from within	• Looks outside the organisation
• Keeps promises	• Doesn't keep promises
• Plain office and facilities	• Lavish office, expensive facilities
• Organisation is top of the agenda	• Self is top of the agenda
• • Sees mistakes as learning opportunities and the opportunity to develop	• Sees mistakes as punishable offences and the means of scapegoating

Peters and Austin additionally state: 'You now know more about leaders and leadership than all the combined graduate business schools in America. You also know whether you have a leader or a non-leader in your manager's office'.

Source From Peters and Austin, *A Passion for Excellence: The Leadership Difference*, Harper and Row (1988).

Conclusions

In business, commercial and public service sector organisations, leadership is that part of management that provides the vision, direction and energy that gives life to policy, strategy and operations. Leadership provides everyone with a point of identity and focus, in relation to the organisation at all times.

Problems always occur when leaders, for whatever reason, are either unwilling or else unable to accept the full responsibilities of the position. Problems are compounded when it becomes known, believed or perceived that the leader is acting without integrity, and is seeking to blame either circumstances or else other people for organisational, strategic and operational shortcomings. In these cases, staff only remain in employment so long as they believe it in their interests to do so; and this invariably leads to the early loss of expert and motivated staff. This in turn can lead to loss of reputation and confidence, as product and output quality falls, and as staff become less willing to deliver high-quality service.

Problems also arise when leaders accept their responsibilities to one group of stakeholders, in preference to others. This is a serious problem in large public service sector and multinational corporations when senior managers discharge their responsibilities to shareholders, political interests and the drives of boards of directors and governors, at the expense of staff, suppliers, customers and clients.

As above, in the world that is emerging from the COVID19 crisis, leadership expertise is going to be ever more highly sought after and valued. Organisations are going to have to change every aspect of their activities, responding to markets and societies that have had their whole patterns of existence and behaviour turned upside down. Organisations are going to have to respond to patterns and structures of work, behaviour and performance that are now in place. All of this is only possible if those in charge are expert and committed to new and ever-evolving ways of conducting effective and sustainable—and profitable—business.

REFERENCES AND FURTHER READING

Adair, J. 1967. *Action Centred Leadership*. Penguin.
Fiedler, F. 1967. *A Theory of Leadership Effectiveness*. McGraw-Hill.
Fiedler, F. 1971. *Leadership*. General Learning Press.
Fiedler, F. 1981. *Leader Attitudes and Group Effectiveness*. Greenwood.
Handy, C.B. 1996. *Understanding Organisations*. Penguin.
Peters, T., and Austin, N. 1988. *A Passion for Excellence: The Leadership Difference*. Harper and Row.

CHAPTER 11

Conclusions

Abstract This chapter summarises an informed view of the present and evolving environment and the pressures that exist and which have to be accommodated. The chapter draws on present and past influential works in the field of management, business and leadership education, identifying the expertise, qualities and approaches necessary if companies and organisations are to deliver effective and profitable activities for the future. Reference is made to the present and envisaged state of activities in the world as it goes on from the COVID19 pandemic, and relates the drives and demands that are certain to be required if successful activities are going to be able to be delivered.

Keywords Transformation · Disruption · The nature of disruption · Leadership development · Developing expertise · Business processes · Leadership repositioning · Repositioning management style · Business transformation

Introduction

The purpose of this chapter is to bring together and summarise the main points raised in full detail in the book. This then in turn forms the foundations for the development of leadership and management expertise. The overall outcome is a much fuller understanding of what leadership and management are (and what they are not); and a much fuller understanding also of the actions needed to develop the foundations of expert and effective organisational practice.

This summary is additionally informed and underpinned by revisiting the work of some of those who were once regarded as the vanguard of organisation and management and leadership development.

Hammer and Champey (1996) attached importance to the value and cost advantages that accrue as the result of paying constant attention to the ways in which business, management and support processes operate in terms of delivering speedy and excellent service, unblocking decision-making pathways. Effective business and management processes rely on clarity, simplicity, speed and security; and this is in direct contrast to many complex organisation hierarchies, that have provided career paths as well as (and in many cases instead of) speed and effectiveness of operations.

Pinchot (1983) defined intrapreneurship as the contribution of entrepreneurial individuals in existing, mature and (often) large corporations. Pinchot described characteristics and traits of intrapreneurs in both behavioural and economic terms: intrapreneurs need to have the specific characteristics of drive, ambition and commitment if they are to succeed. Pinchot stated that creativity and energy were required in every organisation, and not just start ups; all organisations need the drive and commitment of their staff in as many activities as possible. In other words, large corporations require the same dynamic and pioneering approach that is found in new companies.

Speed and clarity of processes, and the emphasis on creativity and energy, will drive organisations into the future, and enable the cost optimisation and effectiveness of product and services delivery required. This means in turn that people with drive and ambition are required to redesign business processes and systems, as well as products and services.

BUSINESS AND ORGANISATION LEADERSHIP

As well as clarity and effectiveness, business and organisation leadership and management additionally require overall understanding and awareness of how the infrastructure, markets, products and services are influenced by social and technological issues. This especially refers to:

- the influence on buyer behaviour of social media;
- reputation management;

- confidence (or lack of) in products and services;
- collective and individual behaviour within organisations;
- behavioural responses to external pressures.

Such issues are either driven or else hindered by the ways in which organisations work. Clarity and effectiveness inform key leadership and managerial choices in the fields of:

- investment appraisal and investment commitments;
- project leadership, direction and management;
- new product and service developments;
- new market and location developments;
- organisation development and staff management.

From this it is essential to be able to evaluate existing and potential staff in terms of their expertise and awareness of how these matters impact their jobs, work and development. This refers to the changing nature of jobs and work as society and technology develop. This means in turn that staff induction, orientation and development programmes need to include:

- statements about work/life balance;
- commitments to change and advancement;
- designed approaches to staff management practices and supervision (of critical importance in the COVID19 and post-pandemic world);
- commitments on all sides to continuous training and development;
- allocations of resources on the basis that underpinning social and technological development is continuous rather than based on a standardised investment appraisal approach which predetermines the returns expected and required before a commitment is made.

The outcome of this is a critical re-evaluation of the commitment required to maximising and optimising the return on the ±65% of capital employed/working capital that is tied up in the staff. It is ever more crucial that the fullest possible attention is made in this area, and that leaders and managers accept this as a condition of being in business.

All of this adds up to a radical repositioning of leadership and management style and approach. It is increasingly difficult to justify traditional scalar chains, reporting relationships and complex promotion and career development pathways that traditional patterns of organisation used to deliver. There is nothing wrong with functional structuring, authority and power; it is how organisations are structured and the power and authority deployed that are the key issues (see box).

Transformation and Disruption

Organisational and managerial transformation and disruption are to be seen from many points of view:

- catalysts for change;
- changing managerial and leadership attitudes;
- expertise development;
- management and leadership buzzwords.

The term 'transformational leadership' is first noted to have been used in 1927 by Mary Parker Follett (Rausch 1991). Follett used the term to describe her fundamentally human approach to the practice of management as 'getting things done through people'.

The ideas have developed as has management practice. As buzzwords, transformational leadership, transformation and disruption have value in terms of getting everyone to start thinking that the present ways of doing things have at least to be questioned and evaluated, even if they are not yet obsolete. It is essential to know and understand that this means attention to every part of the organisation and its products and services and processes. The overall approach required is therefore strategic and inbuilt. Everything is put on the table and evaluated on a continuous basis.

This in turn requires a fundamental rethink of the roles of top and senior managers and organisation leadership. In the UK and many other parts of the world, organisation leadership and direction has largely been concerned with setting strategy and direction and priorities, and then overseeing their implementation. This has now to change. Specific ways of looking at this are:

- from just steering the organisation to being fully involved with its design, activities, markets and staff;
- attending to patterns of activities in every part of the organisation;
- accepting the full range of changes taking place and being fully accountable for their successes and failures;

- deciding who to employ and the conditions under which they are employed;
- evaluating products and services on a continuous basis;
- generating and evaluating new ideas in every area of activities and processes;
- engaging with the staff on a continuous basis;
- engaging with all stakeholders on a continuous basis.

This is all to be underpinned by the key activities of technology integration and the use of data in support of decision-making. Everything that changes and the speed of change in every area needs to be data and technology driven:

- actively, in which data and technology inform what needs to change, when, how and why;
- operationally, in which the effectiveness and efficiency of what is being done is closely monitored as an integral part of environmental scanning and risk management;
- by exception, so that all data and technology is capable of identifying real and potential risks and crises at the earliest possible stage.

THE NATURE OF DISRUPTION

Disruption is the term used to describe any innovation or development that creates a new market and value network and causes existing players in those markets or networks to change or become obsolete (Christensen 1997). The original position was that such disruption was unlikely to come from large and established organisations, as it was in their interests to retain the status quo. As technology has advanced it has become essential for all organisations to become as flexible and dynamic as possible, in whatever sector they exist and operate.

It is also true that some fundamental human needs and especially wants do not change. However people's expectations are constantly being changed and modified and so companies have to be as flexible and as agile as possible in order to establish and define those expectations, and then deliver products and services in ways which both meet and also exceed expectations.

Christensen went on to describe disruption as follows:

- disruption is a process that moves products, services, service, activities and business conduct from the fringe to the mainstream;
- disruption occurs initially in low end (less demanding customers) or new market footholds;
- disruption is identifiable where small scale but viable business activities are being conducted either in low end or new markets.

New companies and new ways of working do not engage with mass markets and customers until the volumes and quality of products and services catch up with the mass market standards. The overall need for universal access to products and services is a major hurdle over which disruptors have to get if they are to permanently or substantially change the face of an industry, sector, location or market.

Success is not a requirement and some businesses can be disruptive but fail. Disruption is therefore a process rather than an event or series of events which have a beginning, middle and end. However successful or otherwise, disruption itself leads to further developments and ideas. This in turn opens up new opportunities, and real and potential uses for technology.

Many small and innovative businesses which show potential are bought out by existing larger players, often at inflated prices. This is so that the large player can control the speed of disruption, and gain as much control as possible over the consequences and opportunities. The large player may also buy up the smaller one to gain a foothold in their market, and to gain access to the customer bases and the information that is held about them, as well as to gain control of the disruptive technology.

Many small and pioneering start ups are bought by larger companies for use as their own incubators or laboratory sections. As well as controlling the outputs and inventions, the larger companies then use the pioneer to test out new products and services, and to evaluate further developments for viability in terms that match existing as well as new business models.

It is likely also that the new firm's business model will differ significantly from incumbent and existing players. The new firm's value proposition above all has to be capable of differentiation so that everyone can see the potential that is on offer. It is also likely that key other parts are recognisably different, so that the whole can be presented as new, better, more convenient and of higher quality as well as delivering products and services and service levels that are of demonstrable real or perceived value to the customer bases.

Relative to existing and major players, the business model needs to deliver on all fronts in terms of:

- cost advantages;
- demonstrable and provable value advantages;
- staff commitment and engagement;
- speed of operation of business processes;
- security and assurance of transactions;
- customer and supplier engagement;
- fixed cost base.

Marginal advantages will also be sought and apparent as the disruptor advances. This again provides incentives for larger companies interested in buying up or buying into the disruptor. Marginal advantages to a large company deliver substantial savings and market access because of their sheer size.

Developing Expertise

The nature of disruption ought to be a key point of inquiry in terms of developing leadership, management and staff expertise. The foundations of this development need to be as above; and then related also to the key issues of continuous improvement, risk management, streamlining of processes and enhanced quality assurance in terms of products, services and service delivery.

This needs to apply to everyone in the organisation. To restrict to top and senior managers and executives is wasteful; organisations need the engagement of everyone in progressing in a disruptive and disrupted environment.

The overall approach required is to use the various approaches as the foundations for developing leadership and managerial expertise. This has to be seen in the social, economic and technological context in which activities and operations are taking place, and of the future that is envisaged.

Any development needs to be managed through active performance management and appraisal processes; and this becomes a core aspect of management and leadership practice. Development and improvement activities need to be fully structured into work, job and occupation patterns; and they need to meet the 4 key criteria for success:

- attention to personal needs, wants, hopes and aspirations;
- attention to professional development
- attention to occupational development;
- attention to organisation needs, wants, drives, priorities and demands.

Development needs to be a core aspect of organisation strategy and an enduring commitment. No organisation or its staff can stand still; everyone who commits to any job or occupation needs to commit to continuous training and development. Those in managerial and key executive positions need to recognise this and to commit the required proportions of organisation resources as a strategic imperative and priority.

This has to be done fully and openly. People who come into organisations need to know that they are committing to this. People presently working within organisations need to know that whatever was done in the past is no longer adequate.

Finally

For all of everything covered here, the main principles and expertise of leadership and management do not change. The context in which the principles and expertise are applied has changed out of all recognition; and unlike previous industrial revolutions these changes have taken place very rapidly, and are being accelerated continuously as the pandemic and post-pandemic world emerges and progresses.

The crucial issue alongside the delivery of the products, services and service is the demand for organisational and management processes. This is because business processes and administrative procedures and organisation structures do not evolve with the service levels and demands. Organisations tend to fit what is required now and for the future, into existing structures and capacities, rather than creating forms and formats which allow themselves to evolve. Above all, at this time, organisations simply cannot afford this, either in purely financial terms, or in terms of the operational cumbersomeness that exists.

All of this in turn requires a fundamental change in the orientation of leadership and management expertise, attitudes and approaches. Leaders and managers who do not recognise the social and technological pressures that are driving these demands are certain to provide less effective services, delivered more slowly and at an ever increasing cost.

With this in mind, processes need to be as simple as possible, while remaining as comprehensive as possible. Companies and organisations in all sectors need to harness and energise the creative expertise of everyone that they employ. New ideas for products, services and service are required all of the time, and these ideas must be capable of proof and evaluation very much more quickly than in the past. Resources and their consumption (and wastage) have to be much more carefully evaluated and assessed; companies and organisations can no longer afford levels of profligacy that were once acceptable.

For industries that are either going to have to grow again, or else completely restructure, the need for expert and committed leadership and management is critical. It is this expertise that is going to steer companies and organisations into the future, as it develops and emerges. It is this expertise also that is going to create and develop the social and economic frameworks and infrastructure on which everyone and everything is going to rely for the immediate and foreseeable future.

REFERENCES AND FURTHER READING

Christensen, C. 1997. *The Innovator's Dilemma: When New Technologies Cause Great Firms to Fail.* Harvard.

Drucker, P.F. 1985. *Innovation and Entrepreneurship.* Harper and Row.

Hammer, M., and J. Champey. 1996. *Re Engineering the Corporation.* Free Press.

Pinchot, G. 1983. *Intrapreneuring.* Wildwood.

Rausch, E.A. 1991. *The Social Construction of Leadership: From Theory to Praxis.* Harper and Row.

Index

A
Adams, T., 83
Alternatives, 49
Amazon, 26, 60
Analysing the environment
   PESTEL, 47, 52
   SPECTACLES, 52, 53
   SWOT, 52
Anthropology, 28
Apple, 39
ASOS, 27
Austin, N., 113, 114

B
Brundtland, G.H., 70
Brundtland report, 70
Business and society, 25, 29

C
Cadbury, 37
Carruthers, S., 83
Cartwright, R., 52
Champey, J., 118

Change, 3, 5, 8–10
Changing face and location of
   population centres, 19
Changing nature of the farming
   industry, 21
Choices, 26–29
Climate change, 71
Clusters, 51
Coca Cola, 39
Colgate, 39
Collaborations, 48
Colloquy
   external, 74, 76
   internal, 73
Competition, 48, 53
Competition at different levels, 48
Contingency leadership, 112
Core strategy, 42
Corporate governance, 82, 87
Corporate social responsibility (CSR),
   82, 89
COVID19, 13, 50, 51, 54, 60, 62,
   66, 77, 106, 115, 119

D
Data, 16, 20, 23
Developing expertise, 123
Disciplines of business, 36, 43

E
Easyjet, 29
Economic environment, 47, 48, 54
Environment, 2–4, 6–9, 13
Essential services, 18, 21
Ethics, 28, 81, 82, 84, 91

F
Fiedler, F., 112
Financial foundation, 29
Financial knowledge and understanding, 3, 10

G
Ghylin, K.M., 64

H
Hamil, J., 83
Hammer, M., 118

I
IBM, 23
Improvement, 7
Inclusion and exclusion, 99–102
Industrial revolutions
 first, 19, 21
 fourth, 20–23, 26–28
 second, 20
 third, 20
Industry and commerce as social infrastructure, 31
Infrastructure, 16, 17, 19–21, 25, 26, 29, 32, 94–96, 99, 101–103
Infrastructure development, 78, 79
IT and technology, 16, 22

K
Key sectors, 77

L
Leaders and non leaders, 113
Leadership, 1–3, 9, 11
 characteristic, 107
 deliverables, 106, 107
 expertise, 106, 107, 111, 115
 position, 106, 107, 111, 112
 qualities, 108, 111
 roles, 110, 111
 styles, 108, 109, 112
 traits, 107
Leadership development, 118
Lewis, John, 37

M
Management as profession, 12
Marketing, 40
Markets, 39
Mary Parker Follett, 120
Miss – selling financial services products, 30
Moore's law, 2

N
New product and service development, 62, 65, 66
Niches, 38, 40
Nissan, 37

O
Obsolescence
 job, 97, 99

organisation, 97, 98
work, 97–99
Open and closed economies, 50
Organisations, 1, 2, 4–9, 12, 13, 45, 46, 48–54
Orthia, L., 95

P
Pandemic, 16, 23
Park Road Fish Bar, 17, 18
Pepsi Cola, 39
Peters, T., 113, 114
Pettinger, R., 60, 64
Pinchot, G., 118
Political changes, 16
Porter, M.E., 38, 50
Production and service delivery, 42
Products and services, 57–63, 65–67
Profit, 3, 5, 6
Psychological contract, 37
Psychology, 28
Public services, 64

Q
Quality
  assurance, 64, 65
  dimensions of quality, 64
  inspection, 65

R
Rational/economic perspective, 27
Rausch, E.A., 120
Relationships
  communities, 86
  staff, 83, 84
  stakeholders, 82, 83
  suppliers, 83, 86
Relationships between business and society, 29
Resources, 3, 4, 6, 7, 9, 10

Responsibilities and obligations
  to communities, 82
  to staff, 82, 84, 85
  to suppliers, 84, 86, 91
Right and wrong, 81, 90
Risk, 9, 11, 12
Ryanair, 26, 29, 39, 58

S
Sachs, J., 70
Samsung, 39
Science fiction, 95
Service levels, 63, 66
Shareholders' interests, 88
Social and economic disruption, 22
Social impacts, 20
Social revolutions, 16
Society, 25, 27, 28, 32
Sociology, 28
Southwestern, 29, 39
Staffing, 41
Standards, 3, 12, 13
  conduct and behaviour, 88, 91
  integrity, 88, 91
  probity, 88
Sternberg, E., 82
Strategy, 37, 38, 72
Supervision, 99, 100
Sustainability
  concerns, 69–71, 79
  definitions, 70
  triple bottom line, 71

T
Technological knowledge and understanding, 9
Technology, 17–21, 23, 24, 83, 85, 89
  assurance, 94, 96, 99
  connectivity, 96, 101, 102
  development, 94–97, 99, 100

    impact on work, 119
    infrastructure, 96, 99, 101, 103
    integration, 96
Transformation, 120
Transformational leadership, 120
Trust, 91

U
Uber, 27
Unilever, 39
Urbanisation, 21

V
Value
    appraisal and reappraisal, 66
    by sector, 61
    confidence, 60, 61
    definitions, 61
    gain and loss, 62
    real and perceived, 61, 62

W
Wage work bargain, 37
Waste
    waste disposal, 72
    waste responsibilities, 77, 79
Wizz, 29, 39
Working
    working remotely, 75
Work life balance, 96

CPI Antony Rowe
Chippenham, UK
2020-10-05 16:42